Expert T-SQL Window Functions in SQL Server

Kathi Kellenberger
with Clayton Groom

Expert T-SQL Window Functions in SQL Server

ISBN-13 (pbk): 978-1-4842-1104-5

ISBN-13 (electronic): 978-1-4842-1103-8

Managing Director: Welmoed Spahr
Lead Editor: Jonathan Gennick
Development Editor: Douglas Pundick
Technical Reviewer: Stéphane Faroult
Editorial Board: Steve Anglin, Mark Beckner, Gary Cornell, Louise Corrigan, Jim DeWolf, Jonathan Gennick, Robert Hutchinson, Michelle Lowman, James Markham, Matthew Moodie, Jeff Olson, Jeffrey Pepper, Douglas Pundick, Ben Renow-Clarke, Gwenan Spearing, Matt Wade, Steve Weiss
Coordinating Editor: Jill Balzano
Copy Editor: Mary Behr
Compositor: SPi Global
Indexer: SPi Global
Artist: SPi Global
Cover Designer: Anna Ishchenko

Distributed to the book trade worldwide by Springer Science+Business Media New York, 233 Spring Street, 6th Floor, New York, NY 10013. Phone 1-800-SPRINGER, fax (201) 348-4505, e-mail orders-ny@springer-sbm.com, or visit www.springeronline.com. Apress Media, LLC is a California LLC and the sole member (owner) is Springer Science + Business Media Finance Inc (SSBM Finance Inc). SSBM Finance Inc is a **Delaware** corporation.

For information on translations, please e-mail rights@apress.com, or visit www.apress.com.

Apress and friends of ED books may be purchased in bulk for academic, corporate, or promotional use. eBook versions and licenses are also available for most titles. For more information, reference our Special Bulk Sales–eBook Licensing web page at www.apress.com/bulk-sales.

Any source code or other supplementary material referenced by the author in this text is available to readers at www.apress.com. For detailed information about how to locate your book's source code, go to www.apress.com/source-code/.

For Gwen.
I have loved watching you grow from a baby into a litte girl.

Contents at a Glance

Contents

About the Authors

Kathi Kellenberger, known to the SQL community as Aunt Kathi, is an independent SQL Server consultant associated with Linchpin People and a SQL Server MVP. She loves writing about SQL Server and has contributed to 11 books as an author, co-author, or technical editor. Kathi enjoys spending free time with family and friends, especially her grandchildren (four and counting!). When she is not working or involved in a game of Hide n Seek with the kids, you may find her at the local karaoke bar. Kathi blogs at auntkathisql.com.

Clayton Groom has over 20 years of in-depth experience creating solutions with the SQL Server product suite. He is an independent BI and analytics consultant specializing in analysis services, data warehouse design, development, optimization, enterprise reporting, and data visualization. His interest and knowledge extends to PerformancePoint, Power Pivot, Power Query, Power Pivot, and configuring Kerberos for SharePoint BI architectures. Clayton is an active PASS member and frequent presenter at the St. Louis SQL Server and MS BI chapters. He can be found on Twitter at @SQLMonger and sometimes blogs at sqlmonger.com.

About the Technical Reviewer

Stéphane Faroult is a French consultant who first discovered relational databases and the SQL language 30 years ago. Stéphane joined Oracle France in its early days (after a brief spell with IBM and a period of time teaching at the University of Ottawa) and developed an interest in performance and tuning topics, on which he soon started writing training courses. After leaving Oracle in 1988, Stéphane briefly tried going straight and did a bit of operational research, but after only a year, he succumbed again to the allure of relational databases. He is currently visiting faculty in the Computing and Information Science department at Kansas State University. For his sins, Stéphane has been performing database consultancy continuously ever since and founded RoughSea Ltd in 1998. In recent years, Stéphane has had a growing interest in education, which has taken various forms, including books (*The Art of SQL*, soon followed by *Refactoring SQL Applications*, both published by O'Reilly) and more recently a textbook (*SQL Success*, published by RoughSea), a series of seminars in Asia, and video tutorials (www.youtube.com/user/roughsealtd).

Acknowledgments

Napolean Hill said that every accomplishment begins with an idea. In this case, I had been presenting window functions at SQL Saturdays, PASS Summit, and other events for a couple of years. When Larry Toothman (@iowatechbear) approached me and said that I should write a book about window functions, I said that I couldn't do it. It's not that I didn't have the material, I just felt that Itzik Ben-Gan's book was the final word on the topic.

Eventually, I realized that I could write this book. Even though I had learned a lot from Itzik, I had discovered many things on my own. Of course, I explain things in a different way than he does. I also realized that there doesn't have to be just one book on any subject. If I look at all the SQL Server books, there are multiple books on any given topic. So, thank you, Larry, for giving me this idea and thank you, Itzik, for teaching me about window functions.

I would also like to thank Clayton Groom for writing a fantastic chapter to end the book. I ran into Clayton at a user group meeting and mentioned that I was writing a book. By the time we left the building, a deal was made.

Of course, writing a book takes a village. Thank you to everyone at Apress who had any role in shaping this book, especially Jonathan Gennick and Jill Balzano. Also thanks to editors Stéphane Faroult and Mary Behr.

Thank you to my family, especially Dennis, who takes care of everything for me so that I can live this crazy life full of adventures like writing books. Thank you to my children, their spouses, my grandchildren, my parents, and my siblings for understanding when I am busy.

Finally, I must thank the most important person of all, and that is you, the one reading this book. Without you, there is no reason at all to write it. I hope that you enjoy learning from me.

Author's Note

I began using the ROW_NUMBER function ten years ago while not even realizing it was a window function. I didn't hear the term "window function" until SQL Server 2012 was announced. Since then, I've also seen "windowing" and "windowed" to describe these functions. For the sake of simplicity, this book will refer to them as "window functions."

▓ ▓ ▓

CHAPTER 1

Looking Through the Window

SQL Server is a powerful database platform with a versatile query language called T-SQL. The most exciting T-SQL enhancement over the past decade is, without a doubt, window functions. Window functions enable you to solve query problems in new, easier ways, and with better performance most of the time.

After the release of SQL Server 2000, SQL Server enthusiasts waited five long years for the next version of SQL Server to arrive. Microsoft delivered an entirely new product with SQL Server 2005. This version brought SQL Server Management Studio, SQL Server Integration Services, snapshot isolation, and database mirroring. Microsoft also enhanced T-SQL with many great features, such as Common Table Expressions (CTEs). The most exciting T-SQL enhancement of all with 2005 was the introduction of window functions.

That was just the beginning. Window functions are part of the ANSI Standard SQL specification, and more functionality according to the standard was released with version 2012 of SQL Server. Even now, the functionality falls short of the entire specification, so there is more to look forward to in the future.

This chapter provides a first look at two T-SQL window functions, LAG and ROW_NUMBER. You will learn just what the window is and how to define it with the OVER clause. You will also learn how to divide the windows into smaller sections called partitions.

Discovering Window Functions

Window functions do not let you do anything that was impossible to do with earlier functionality, and they have nothing to do with the Microsoft Windows API. Using previously available methods, such as self joins, correlated subqueries, and cursors, you can solve just about any T-SQL problem if you work at it long and hard enough. The main benefit of window functions is the ease in which you can solve these tricky queries. Most of the time, you also realize a big boost in performance over the older methods. You can often use a window function to change a solution involving many statements or subqueries to one easier statement.

Window functions can be divided into several categories: ranking functions, window aggregates, accumulating window aggregates, offset functions, and statistical functions. You can use these functions to assign a rank to each row, calculate summary values without grouping, calculate running totals, include columns from different rows in your results, and calculate percentages over a group. You'll learn about these functions as you read this book.

My favorite window function is called LAG. It is one of the offset functions, which you will learn about in Chapter 7. LAG allows you to include any column from a different row in your results. Using LAG is easier and performs better than older methods that do the same thing.

Within the same year (just a few months apart), two different people approached me for help with essentially the same problem: using data from the stock market, how can one compare the closing price of a stock from one day to the next? The traditional solution requires that each row of the data be joined to the prior row to get the closing price from the previous day. By using the LAG function, the solution is not only simpler to write, it also performs much better.

▧ **Note**　If you would like to follow along with this example, a sample database with the stock market data can be found along with the code for this chapter on the Apress site.

For a quick look at how to solve this problem using one of the traditional methods and by using LAG, review and run Listing 1-1.

Listing 1-1.　Two Approaches to Solving the Stock Market Problem

```
USE StockAnalysis;
GO
--1-1.1 Using a subquery
SELECT TickerSymbol, TradeDate, ClosePrice,
    (SELECT TOP(1) ClosePrice
    FROM StockHistory AS SQ
    WHERE SQ.TickerSymbol  = OQ.TickerSymbol
        AND SQ.TradeDate < OQ.TradeDate
    ORDER BY TradeDate DESC) AS PrevClosePrice
FROM StockHistory AS OQ
ORDER BY TickerSymbol, TradeDate;

--1-1.2 Using LAG
SELECT TickerSymbol, TradeDate, ClosePrice,
    LAG(ClosePrice) OVER(PARTITION BY TickerSymbol
            ORDER BY TradeDate) AS PrevClosePrice
FROM StockHistory
ORDER BY TickerSymbol, TradeDate;
```

The partial results are shown in Figure 1-1. Query 1 uses a correlated subquery to select one ClosePrice for every outer row. By joining the TickerSymbol from the inner query to the outer query you ensure that you are not comparing two different stocks. The inner and outer queries are also joined by the TradeDate, but the TradeDate for the inner query must be less than the outer query to make sure you get a prior day. The inner query must also be sorted to get the row that has the latest data but still less than the current date. This query took six seconds to run on my laptop, which has 8GB of RAM and is using SSD storage. A total of 181,946 rows were returned.

	TickerSymbol	TradeDate	ClosePrice	PrevClosePrice
1	AA	2013-12-02	9.55	NULL
2	AA	2013-12-03	9.42	9.55
3	AA	2013-12-04	9.36	9.42
4	AA	2013-12-05	9.35	9.36
5	AA	2013-12-06	9.36	9.35
6	AA	2013-12-09	9.48	9.36

	TickerSymbol	TradeDate	ClosePrice	PrevClosePrice
1	AA	2013-12-02	9.55	NULL
2	AA	2013-12-03	9.42	9.55
3	AA	2013-12-04	9.36	9.42
4	AA	2013-12-05	9.35	9.36
5	AA	2013-12-06	9.36	9.35
6	AA	2013-12-09	9.48	9.36

Figure 1-1. *Partial results of the Stock Market problem*

Query 2 uses the window function LAG to solve the same problem and produces the same results. Don't worry about the syntax at this point; you will be an expert by the end of this book. The query using LAG took just two seconds to run on my laptop.

By just looking at the code in Listing 1-1, you can see that Query 2 using LAG is much simpler to write, even though you may not understand the syntax just yet. It also runs much faster because it is just reading the table once instead of once per row like Query 1. As you continue reading this book and running the examples, you will learn how window functions like LAG will make your life easier and your customers happier!

Thinking About the Window

Window functions are different than regular functions because they operate over a set of rows, also called a *window*. This may sound similar to aggregate queries. Aggregate functions, such as SUM and AVG, operate on groups of rows and provide summary values.

When you write an aggregate query, you lose the detail columns. Adding detail columns back into an aggregate query forces you to include those columns in a GROUP BY clause. You can only get the details for those columns listed in the GROUP BY clause.

When adding a GROUP BY clause, instead of returning a summary over all the rows, you will see multiple summary lines, one for each unique set of GROUP BY columns. For example, to get a count of the all the rows using an aggregate query, you must leave out the other columns. Once you add columns into the SELECT and GROUP BY, you get a count for each unique grouping, not the entire set of results.

Queries with window functions are much different than traditional aggregate queries. There are no restrictions to the columns that appear in the SELECT list, and no GROUP BY clause is required. Instead of summary rows being returned, all of the details are returned and the result of the expression with the window function is included as just another column. In fact, by using a window function to get the overall count of the rows, you could still include all of the columns in the table.

Imagine looking through a window to see a specific set of rows while your query is running. You have one last chance to perform an operation, such as grabbing one of the columns. The result of the operation is added as an additional column. You will learn how window functions really work as you read this book, but the idea of looking through the window has helped me understand and explain window functions to audiences at many SQL Server events. Figure 1-2 illustrates this concept.

The Window

	TickerSymbol	TradeDate	ClosePrice
1	AA	2013-12-02	9.55
2	AA	2013-12-03	9.42
3	AA	2013-12-04	9.36
4	AA	2013-12-05	9.35
5	AA	2013-12-06	9.36

TickerSymbol	TradeDate	ClosePrice	OpenPrice
AA	2013-12-02	9.55	9.62
AA	2013-12-03	9.42	9.53

Figure 1-2. Looking through the window to perform an operation on a set of rows

The window is not limited to the columns found in the SELECT list of the query. For example, if you take a look at the StockHistory table, you will see that there is also an OpenPrice column. The OpenPrice from one day is not the same as the ClosePrice from the previous day. If you wanted to, you could use LAG to include the previous OpenPrice in the results even though it is not included in the SELECT list originally.

In the stock history example using LAG, each row has its own window. When the calculation is performed on the third row of the data, the window consists of the second and third rows. When the calculation is performed on the fourth row, the window consists of the third and fourth rows.

What would happen if the rows for 2013-12-02 were filtered out of the query? Does the window contain filtered-out rows? The answer is "No," which brings up two very important concepts to understand when using window functions: where window functions may be used in the query and the logical order of operations.

Window functions may only be used in the SELECT list and ORDER BY clause. You cannot filter or group on window functions. In situations where you must filter or group on the results of a window function, the solution is to separate the logic using a derived table subquery or CTE and filter or group in the outer query.

Window functions operate logically after the FROM, WHERE, GROUP BY, and HAVING clauses. They operate logically before the TOP and DISTINCT clauses are evaluated. Figure 1-3 illustrates the order of operations. You will learn more about how DISTINCT and TOP affect queries with window functions in the "Uncovering Special Case Windows" section later in this chapter.

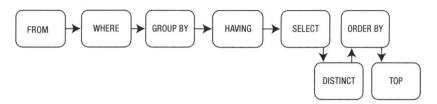

Figure 1-3. *The order of operations including window functions*

The window is defined by the OVER clause. Notice in Query 1 of Listing 1-1 that the LAG function is followed by an OVER clause. Each type of window function has specific requirements for the OVER clause. The LAG function must have an ORDER BY expression and may have a PARTITION BY expression.

Understanding the OVER Clause

One thing that sets window functions apart is the OVER clause, which defines the window or set. Without exception, window functions will have an OVER clause. In some cases, the OVER clause will be empty. You will see empty OVER clauses in Chapter 3 when working with window aggregate functions.

▒ **Note**   There is one situation in which you will see the OVER keyword in a query not following a window function, and that is with the sequence object. The sequence object, introduced with SQL Server 2008, is a bucket containing incrementing numbers often used in place of an identity column.

For any type of expression in the SELECT list of a query, a calculation is performed for each row in the results. For example, if you had a query with the expression Col1 + Col2, those two columns would be added together once for every row returned. A calculation is performed for row 1, row 2, row 3, and so on. Expressions with window functions must also be calculated once per row. In this case, however, the expressions operate over a set that can be different for each row.

The OVER clause determines which rows make up the window. The OVER clause has three possible components: PARTITION BY, ORDER BY, and the frame. The ORDER BY expression is required for some types of window functions. Where it is used, it determines the order in which the window function is applied.

Many T-SQL developers have used the ROW_NUMBER function. They may not have even realized that this is one of the window functions. ROW_NUMBER supplies an incrementing number, starting with one, for each row. The order in which the numbers are applied is determined by the columns specified in the ORDER BY expression, which is independent of an ORDER BY clause in the query itself. Run the queries in Listing 1-2 to see how this works.

Listing 1-2. Applying the Row Numbers to Different Columns

```
USE AdventureWorks;
GO
--1-2.1 Row numbers applied by CustomerID
SELECT CustomerID, SalesOrderID,
    ROW_NUMBER() OVER(ORDER BY CustomerID) AS RowNumber
FROM Sales.SalesOrderHeader;

--1-2.2 Row numbers applied by SalesOrderID
SELECT CustomerID, SalesOrderID,
    ROW_NUMBER() OVER(ORDER BY SalesOrderID) AS RowNumber
FROM Sales.SalesOrderHeader;
```

▓ **Note**   The AdventureWorks and AdventureWorksDW databases are used in the examples throughout this book. Both the 2012 and 2014 versions will work with the examples. If you are using the 2012 version, the dates within the data will be different than shown here. Queries filtering on dates will need to be adjusted.

The OVER clause follows the ROW_NUMBER function. Inside the OVER clause, you will see ORDER BY followed by one or more columns. The difference between Queries 1 and 2 is just the ORDER BY expression within the OVER clause. Notice in the partial results shown in Figure 1-4 that the row numbers end up applied in the order of the column found in the ORDER BY expression of the OVER clause, which is also the order that the data is returned. Since the data must be sorted to apply the row numbers, it is easy for the data to stay in that order, but it is not guaranteed. The only way to actually guarantee the order of the results is to add an ORDER BY to the query.

	CustomerID	SalesOrderID	RowNumber
1	11000	43793	1
2	11000	51522	2
3	11000	57418	3
4	11001	43767	4
5	11001	51493	5
6	11001	72773	6

	CustomerID	SalesOrderID	RowNumber
1	29825	43659	1
2	29672	43660	2
3	29734	43661	3
4	29994	43662	4
5	29565	43663	5
6	29898	43664	6

Figure 1-4. *Partial results of using ROW_NUMBER with different OVER clauses*

If the query itself has an ORDER BY clause, it can be different than the ORDER BY within OVER. Listing 1-3 demonstrates.

Listing 1-3. Using ROW_NUMBER with a Different ORDER BY in the OVER Clause

```
--1-3.1 Row number with a different ORDER BY
SELECT CustomerID, SalesOrderID,
    ROW_NUMBER() OVER(ORDER BY CustomerID) AS RowNumber
FROM Sales.SalesOrderHeader
ORDER BY SalesOrderID;
```

In this case, the row numbers are applied in order of the CustomerID, but the results are returned in order of SalesOrderID. The partial results are shown in Figure 1-5. In order to show that the row numbers are applied correctly, the figure shows the grid scrolled down to the first customer, CustomerID 11000.

	CustomerID	SalesOrderID	RowNumber
135	11000	43793	1
136	11029	43794	87
137	27615	43795	25629
138	17956	43796	13624
139	16345	43797	11181

Figure 1-5. *Partial results of showing a query with a different ORDER BY than the OVER clause*

Just like the ORDER BY clause of a query, you can specify a descending order with the DESCENDING or DESC keyword within the OVER clause, as shown in Listing 1-4.

Listing 1-4. Using ROW_NUMBER with a Descending ORDER BY

```
--1-4.1 Row number with a descending ORDER BY
SELECT CustomerID, SalesOrderID,
    ROW_NUMBER() OVER(ORDER BY CustomerID DESC) AS RowNumber
FROM Sales.SalesOrderHeader;
```

Figure 1-6 shows partial results. Since it was easy for the database engine to return the results in descending order by CustomerID, you can easily see that row number one was applied to the highest CustomerID.

	CustomerID	SalesOrderID	RowNumber
1	30118	71803	1
2	30118	65221	2
3	30118	58928	3
4	30118	53480	4
5	30118	50675	5
6	30118	49499	6

Figure 1-6. *Partial results of ROW_NUMBER with a descending ORDER BY*

In the SalesOrderHeader table, the CustomerID is not unique. Notice in the last example that 30113 is the largest CustomerID. The row number with SalesOrderID 71803 is 1 and with 65221 is 2. There is no guarantee that the row numbers will be lined up exactly this way. To ensure that the row numbers line up as expected, use a unique column or combination of columns in the ORDER BY expression of the OVER clause. If you use more than one column, separate the columns with commas. You could even apply the row numbers in a random order. Listing 1-5 demonstrates this.

Listing 1-5. Using a Random Order with ROW_NUMBER

```
--1-5.1 Row number with a random ORDER BY
SELECT CustomerID, SalesOrderID,
    ROW_NUMBER() OVER(ORDER BY NEWID()) AS RowNumber
FROM Sales.SalesOrderHeader;
```

By using the NEWID function, the row numbers are applied in a random fashion. Figure 1-7 shows this. If you run the code, you will see different CustomerID values lined up with the row numbers. Each time the data is returned in order of row number, just because it is easy to do so.

	CustomerID	SalesOrderID	RowNumber
1	26829	73862	1
2	19904	46515	2
3	29145	45189	3
4	30092	59067	4
5	25029	49245	5
6	13514	44011	6

Figure 1-7. *Partial results of ROW_NUMBER with a random ORDER BY*

As you may guess, applying the row numbers in a specific order involves sorting, which is an expensive operation. If you wish to generate row numbers but do not care about the order, you can use a subquery selecting a literal value in place of a column name. Listing 1-6 demonstrates how to do this.

Listing 1-6. Using ROW_NUMBER with No Order

```
--1-6.1 Use a constant for an ORDER BY
SELECT CustomerID, SalesOrderID,
    ROW_NUMBER() OVER(ORDER BY (SELECT 1)) AS RowNumber
FROM Sales.SalesOrderHeader;

--1-6.2 Apply an ORDER BY to the query
SELECT CustomerID, SalesOrderID,
    ROW_NUMBER() OVER(ORDER BY (SELECT 1)) AS RowNumber
FROM Sales.SalesOrderHeader
ORDER BY SalesOrderID;

--1-6.3 No ROW_NUMBER and no ORDER BY
SELECT CustomerID, SalesOrderID
FROM Sales.SalesOrderHeader;
```

Figure 1-8 shows the partial results. To accomplish this, a subquery selecting a constant replaces the ORDER BY column. In Queries 1 and 2, the OVER clauses are identical, but the row numbers are applied differently, the easiest way possible. The easiest way is the order that the results would be returned even if the ROW_NUMBER function was not there. Query 3 shows how the rows are returned with no ROW_NUMBER and no ORDER BY. You may be wondering why the optimizer chose to return the results in Queries 1 and 3 in CustomerID order. There just happens to be a nonclustered index on CustomerID covering those queries. The optimizer chose the index that is ordered on CustomerID to solve the queries.

	CustomerID	SalesOrderID	RowNumber
1	11000	43793	1
2	11000	51522	2
3	11000	57418	3
4	11001	43767	4

	CustomerID	SalesOrderID	RowNumber
1	29825	43659	1
2	29672	43660	2
3	29734	43661	3
4	29994	43662	4

	CustomerID	SalesOrderID
1	11000	43793
2	11000	51522
3	11000	57418
4	11001	43767

Figure 1-8. *Partial results of letting the engine decide how row numbers are applied*

Another thing to learn from this example is that ROW_NUMBER is nondeterministic. It is not guaranteed to return the identical values under the same situations. By checking the article "Deterministic and Nondeterministic Functions" in SQL Server Books Online, you will find that ROW_NUMBER, along with the other window functions, are nondeterministic. You may argue that this is wrong because a different ORDER BY is used for the two queries, causing the two ROW_NUMBER functions to have different inputs. Books Online states:

> *You cannot influence the determinism of any built-in function. Each built-in function is deterministic or nondeterministic based on how the function is implemented by SQL Server. For example, specifying an ORDER BY clause in a query does not change the determinism of a function that used in that query.*

There are a couple of things that you cannot do with window functions that may be related to determinism. You cannot use a window function expression in a computed column, and you cannot use a window function expression as a key for the clustered index of a view.

The ORDER BY expression in the OVER clause is pretty versatile. You can use an expression instead of a column for the ORDER BY expression of the OVER clause. You can also list multiple columns or expressions. Listing 1-7 demonstrates these concepts.

Listing 1-7. Using an Expression in the ORDER BY and Another Column

```
--1-7.1 Use an expression in the ORDER BY
SELECT CustomerID, SalesOrderID, OrderDate,
    ROW_NUMBER() OVER(ORDER BY CASE WHEN OrderDate > '2013/12/31'
        THEN 0 ELSE 1 END, SalesOrderID) AS RowNumber
FROM Sales.SalesOrderHeader;
```

Figure 1-9 shows partial results. In this case, the row numbers are applied first to the orders from 2014, then by SalesOrderID. The grid is scrolled down to the last three orders of 2014 so you can see that the next numbers applied are from the beginning of the data, 2011.

	CustomerID	SalesOrderID	OrderDate	RowNumber
11759	15251	75121	2014-06-30 00:00:00.000	11759
11760	15868	75122	2014-06-30 00:00:00.000	11760
11761	18759	75123	2014-06-30 00:00:00.000	11761
11762	29825	43659	2011-05-31 00:00:00.000	11762
11763	29672	43660	2011-05-31 00:00:00.000	11763
11764	29734	43661	2011-05-31 00:00:00.000	11764

Figure 1-9. Partial results of using an expression and another column

There are two additional components of the OVER clause: partitioning and framing. You will learn about framing, introduced in 2012, in Chapter 6. Partitioning divides the window into multiple, smaller windows.

Dividing Windows with Partitions

If there happens to be a window in the room you are sitting in, take a look at it now. Is it one large piece of glass, or is it divided into smaller panes? A window that is divided into panes is still a window. Each individual pane is also a window.

The same concept applies to window functions. The entire set of results is the window, but you can also divide the set up into smaller windows based on one or more columns. The OVER clause contains an optional component, PARTITION BY. When a PARTTITION BY is not supplied, the partition is the larger window.

The query using LAG to solve the stock market problem partitioned the data by the TickerSymbol column. By separating the data by TickerSymbol, the ClosePrice from one stock was not retrieved by rows of another stock. In the case of the ROW_NUMBER function demonstrated earlier in this chapter, you can force the numbers to start over at 1 for each partition. Listing 1-8 demonstrates this feature.

Listing 1-8. Using PARTITION BY

```
--1-8.1 Use ROW_NUMBER with PARTITION BY
SELECT CustomerID, SalesOrderID,
    ROW_NUMBER() OVER(PARTITION BY CustomerID ORDER BY SalesOrderID)
    AS RowNumber
FROM Sales.SalesOrderHeader;
```

Figure 1-10 shows partial results. Notice that the row numbers start over at one for each customer.

	CustomerID	SalesOrderID	RowNumber
1	11000	43793	1
2	11000	51522	2
3	11000	57418	3
4	11001	43767	1
5	11001	51493	2
6	11001	72773	3
7	11002	43736	1

Figure 1-10. *Partial results of using the PARTITION BY option with ROW_NUMBER*

The PARTITION BY expression of the OVER clause is supported by all window functions. It is also always optional. If the PARTITION BY is left out, any and all rows could be included in the window. When the PARTITION BY is used, each window may only consist of the rows matching the PARTITION BY column or columns.

Uncovering Special Case Windows

So far the examples have been pretty straightforward, but there are some situations that are counterintuitive if you don't know what is going on. The examples in this section use the ROW_NUMBER function, but the concepts apply to any window function.

First, take a look at what happens when the DISTINCT keyword is used with ROW_NUMBER. The window function operates before DISTINCT, which can lead to results you may not expect. Listing 1-9 demonstrates using DISTINCT with ROW_NUMBER to get a list of the unique OrderDates along with a row number.

Listing 1-9. Using DISTINCT with ROW_NUMBER

```
--1-9.1 Using DISTINCT
SELECT DISTINCT OrderDate,
    ROW_NUMBER() OVER(ORDER BY OrderDate) AS RowNumber
FROM Sales.SalesOrderHeader
ORDER BY RowNumber;

--1-9.2 Separate logic with CTE
WITH OrderDates AS (
    SELECT DISTINCT OrderDate
    FROM Sales.SalesOrderHeader)
SELECT OrderDate,
    ROW_NUMBER() OVER(ORDER BY OrderDate) AS RowNumber
FROM OrderDates
ORDER BY RowNumber;
```

Figure 1-11 shows the partial results. Query 1 returns 31,465 rows, one row for every order in the table even though many orders have the same date. This is definitely not the intended answer. The row numbers are generated before DISTINCT is applied. Because the row numbers are unique, every row in the results ends up being unique and DISTINCT cannot eliminate any rows. Query 2 demonstrates the solution: get a distinct list of the order dates first in a CTE, and then apply the row numbers in the outer query. Query 2 returns 1124 rows, the number of unique order dates. You could also use a temp table, a table variable, a view, or a derived table to create the distinct list first.

	OrderDate	RowNumber
1	2011-05-31 00:00:00.000	1
2	2011-05-31 00:00:00.000	2
3	2011-05-31 00:00:00.000	3
4	2011-05-31 00:00:00.000	4
5	2011-05-31 00:00:00.000	5
6	2011-05-31 00:00:00.000	6
7	2011-05-31 00:00:00.000	7
8	2011-05-31 00:00:00.000	8

	OrderDate	RowNumber
1	2011-05-31 00:00:00.000	1
2	2011-06-01 00:00:00.000	2
3	2011-06-02 00:00:00.000	3
4	2011-06-03 00:00:00.000	4
5	2011-06-04 00:00:00.000	5
6	2011-06-05 00:00:00.000	6
7	2011-06-06 00:00:00.000	7
8	2011-06-07 00:00:00.000	8

Figure 1-11. Partial results of using DISTINCT with ROW_NUMBER

You will also find interesting behavior when you use TOP. Once again, the row numbers are generated before TOP is applied. I first discovered this when I was inserting random rows into a table for some unit tests. The idea was to reinsert a sample of rows back into the same table with new ID numbers. To generate the new IDs, I wanted to add row numbers to the maximum existing ID. Since I wanted to insert a specific number of rows, I used TOP. Instead of the row numbers starting with one as I expected, they started with a random value. Listing 1-10 shows how using TOP can affect window functions.

Listing 1-10. Using TOP with ROW_NUMBER

```
--1-10.1 Using TOP with ROW_NUMBER
SELECT TOP(6) CustomerID, SalesOrderID,
    ROW_NUMBER() OVER(ORDER BY SalesOrderID) AS RowNumber
FROM Sales.SalesOrderHeader
ORDER BY NEWID();
```

```
--1-10.2 Separate the logic with a CTE
WITH Orders AS (
    SELECT TOP(6) CustomerID, SalesOrderID
    FROM Sales.SalesOrderHeader
    ORDER BY NEWID())
SELECT CustomerID, SalesOrderID,
    ROW_NUMBER() OVER(ORDER BY SalesOrderID) AS RowNumber
FROM Orders;
```

Figure 1-12 shows the results. If you run this example, you will see different random results. The purpose of the example is to generate random rows with a row number starting with one. Query 1 returns row numbers, but they are random. By using a CTE to separate the logic, TOP can operate first. Query 2 returns a random set of rows, but the row numbers start with one.

	CustomerID	SalesOrderID	RowNumber
1	15734	71756	28098
2	17977	50165	6507
3	15575	72626	28968
4	30086	63172	19514
5	23777	57297	13639
6	12314	49330	5672

	CustomerID	SalesOrderID	RowNumber
1	27920	43996	1
2	25226	51025	2
3	28084	65819	3
4	13356	68499	4
5	17453	71538	5
6	12330	73865	6

Figure 1-12. *The results of using TOP with ROW_NUMBER*

The final interesting situation involves adding window functions to aggregate queries. This functionality is covered in Chapter 3 in the "Adding Window Aggregates to Aggregate Queries" section.

Summary

Window functions, added with SQL Server 2005 and 2012, provide new, easy ways to solve challenging queries. Window functions are part of the ANSI standards for SQL. The standards committee has defined even more functionality, so it's possible that Microsoft may include additional functions in the future. Window functions must include an OVER clause, which defines the window for each row to operate on. Depending on the window function used, the OVER clause may contain ORDER BY, PARTITION BY, and frame expressions. In many cases, using a window function has better performance over older methods.

Now that you understand the basics of window functions, it is time to investigate ranking functions. In Chapter 2, you will learn how to use the four ranking functions introduced with SQL Server 2005 to solve challenging T-SQL queries.

CHAPTER 2

▓ ▓ ▓

Discovering Ranking Functions

The four ranking functions were introduced to T-SQL by Microsoft in 2005. Three of the functions, ROW_NUMBER, RANK, and DENSE_RANK, assign a sequential number to each row in a query's results. The fourth ranking function, NTILE, divides the rows by assigning a bucket number to the each row in the results. The group of low ranking rows gets an NTILE value of one while the highest ranking group of rows is assigned the top number.

While adding a number to a row is not generally the answer in itself, this functionality is often the basis for many solutions. This chapter shows how to use the four ranking functions and how to apply them to some real-world problems.

Using ROW_NUMBER

Based on my asking audiences at SQL Server events around the United States, ROW_NUMBER is the most well-known and commonly used window function. Many SQL Server professionals admit to using ROW_NUMBER even if they do not realize it is one of the window functions. You saw ROW_NUMBER in action in Chapter 1 when you learned about the OVER clause. Now you will take an even deeper look at ROW_NUMBER.

The ROW_NUMBER function returns a unique integer starting with one for each row in the window. An ORDER BY expression inside the OVER clause is required, and it determines the order in which the numbers are applied. All of the window functions support an optional PARTITION BY expression that divides the window into smaller sets. The row number for each partition begins with one and increments by one. Here is the basic syntax for ROW_NUMBER, which may appear in the SELECT list and ORDER BY clause of a query:

```
ROW_NUMBER() OVER([PARTITION BY <col1>[,<col2>,...<n>]]
ORDER BY <col3>[,<col4>])
```

Listing 2-1 demonstrates ROW_NUMBER with and without a PARTITION BY expression. So that the row numbers line up by CustomerID for comparison, the ORDER BY expressions of the OVER clause are different.

Listing 2-1. Using ROW_NUMBER with and without a PARTITION BY

```
USE AdventureWorks;
GO
--2-1.1 Using ROW_NUMBER with and without a PARTITION BY
SELECT CustomerID, FORMAT(OrderDate,'yyyy-MM-dd')
    AS OrderDate, SalesOrderID,
    ROW_NUMBER() OVER(PARTITION BY CustomerID ORDER BY SalesOrderID)
        AS WithPart,
    ROW_NUMBER() OVER(ORDER BY CustomerID) AS WithoutPart
FROM Sales.SalesOrderHeader;
```

Figure 2-1 shows the partial results. The row number columns, WithPart and WithoutPart, are the same values for the first three rows, CustomerID 11000. After that, the WithPart rows start over for each new CustomerID.

	CustomerID	OrderDate	SalesOrderID	WithPart	WithoutPart
1	11000	2011-06-21	43793	1	1
2	11000	2013-06-20	51522	2	2
3	11000	2013-10-03	57418	3	3
4	11001	2011-06-17	43767	1	4
5	11001	2013-06-18	51493	2	5
6	11001	2014-05-12	72773	3	6
7	11002	2011-06-09	43736	1	7
8	11002	2013-06-02	51238	2	8

Figure 2-1. *Partial results of ROW_NUMBER with and without partitioning*

The OVER clause in Query 2 is not unique. The row numbers for SalesOrderID 43793 each return 1. It's possible for the WithoutPart value to be 2 or 3 since there are three orders for CustomerID 11000. The row numbers are applied correctly since they are in order of CustomerID, but since CustomerID is not unique, the way the numbers are applied within CustomerID has more to do with luck or possibly the current implementation of the database engine. Listing 2-2 shows how different row numbers are possible with the same OVER clause.

Listing 2-2. Different Row Numbers with the Same OVER Clause

```
--2-2.1 Query ORDER BY ascending
SELECT CustomerID, OrderDate, SalesOrderID,
    ROW_NUMBER() OVER(ORDER BY CustomerID) AS RowNumber
FROM Sales.SalesOrderHeader
ORDER BY CustomerID, SalesOrderID;
```

```
--2-2.2 Query ORDER BY descending
SELECT CustomerID, OrderDate, SalesOrderID,
    ROW_NUMBER() OVER(ORDER BY CustomerID) AS RowNumber
FROM Sales.SalesOrderHeader
ORDER BY CustomerID, SalesOrderID DESC;
```

Figure 2-2 shows the partial results. The OVER clauses are identical, but the queries are sorted differently. The row number for SalesOrderID 43793 in Query 1 is 1, but the row number is 3 in Query 2.

	CustomerID	OrderDate	SalesOrderID	RowNumber
1	11000	2011-06-21 00:00:00.000	43793	1
2	11000	2013-06-20 00:00:00.000	51522	2
3	11000	2013-10-03 00:00:00.000	57418	3
4	11001	2011-06-17 00:00:00.000	43767	4

	CustomerID	OrderDate	SalesOrderID	RowNumber
1	11000	2013-10-03 00:00:00.000	57418	1
2	11000	2013-06-20 00:00:00.000	51522	2
3	11000	2011-06-21 00:00:00.000	43793	3
4	11001	2014-05-12 00:00:00.000	72773	4

Figure 2-2. *Different results with nonunique ORDER BY in the OVER clause*

This proves that ROW_NUMBER is nondetermistic; in other words, you can get different values from the function under the same circumstances. The ORDER BY clause of the query doesn't affect determinism, so this is a valid test.

To ensure repeatable results when using ROW_NUMBER, actually with any of the window functions, make sure that the ORDER BY columns in the OVER clause are unique. Listing 2-3 is an example using multiple ORDER BY columns so that the expression is unique.

Listing 2-3. Using Multiple Columns in the ORDER BY Expression to Ensure Uniqueness

```
--2-3.1 Using ROW_NUMBER a unique ORDER BY
SELECT CustomerID, OrderDate, SalesOrderID,
    ROW_NUMBER() OVER(ORDER BY CustomerID, SalesOrderID) AS RowNum
FROM Sales.SalesOrderHeader
ORDER BY CustomerID, SalesOrderID;

--2-3.2 Change to descending
SELECT CustomerID, OrderDate, SalesOrderID,
    ROW_NUMBER() OVER(ORDER BY CustomerID, SalesOrderID) AS RowNum
FROM Sales.SalesOrderHeader
ORDER BY CustomerID, SalesOrderID DESC;
```

Figure 2-3 shows the partial results. In this case, SaleOrderID is 43793 has a row number of 1 regardless of the query's ORDER BY clause. ROW_NUMBER is still a nondeterministic function, but the assignments are consistent because of the unique ORDER BY columns.

	CustomerID	OrderDate	SalesOrderID	RowNum
1	11000	2011-06-21 00:00:00.000	43793	1
2	11000	2013-06-20 00:00:00.000	51522	2
3	11000	2013-10-03 00:00:00.000	57418	3
4	11001	2011-06-17 00:00:00.000	43767	4
5	11001	2013-06-18 00:00:00.000	51493	5
6	11001	2014-05-12 00:00:00.000	72773	6

	CustomerID	OrderDate	SalesOrderID	RowNum
1	11000	2013-10-03 00:00:00.000	57418	3
2	11000	2013-06-20 00:00:00.000	51522	2
3	11000	2011-06-21 00:00:00.000	43793	1
4	11001	2014-05-12 00:00:00.000	72773	6
5	11001	2013-06-18 00:00:00.000	51493	5
6	11001	2011-06-17 00:00:00.000	43767	4

Figure 2-3. *Using a unique ORDER BY expression of the OVER clause*

It is also possible to have multiple columns, expressions, and subqueries in the PARTITION BY expression of the OVER clause. In fact, as you will see in the "Solving Queries with Ranking Functions" section at the end of this chapter, multiple columns in the PARTITION BY is the key to solving some real-world examples.

With ROW_NUMBER, the engine sorts the rows in each partition and assigns unique numbers based on the position of each row. You have seen situations where the ORDER BY expression of OVER is not unique, so the row numbers are not guaranteed to line up exactly the same each time when there are ties in the values. Now you will learn about two functions that handle ties differently: RANK and DENSE_RANK.

Understanding RANK and DENSE_RANK

The functions RANK and DENSE_RANK look very similar to ROW_NUMBER. In fact, in many queries they will return exactly the same values as ROW_NUMBER. The RANK and DENSE_RANK functions are quite different, however, since instead of just assigning sequential numbers, they actually rank the rows based on the ORDER BY expression.

The difference shows up when the ORDER BY column of the OVER clause is not unique. For example, many customers could place orders on the same date, but each order has a unique OrderID. If you used the OrderDate column instead of the OrderID, you will see ties in the results. The ranking of the rows with ties will be the same.

There is also a difference between RANK and DENSE_RANK. The RANK function returns the rank of the current row compared to all the rows of the partition. The DENSE_RANK function returns the unique rank of the current row in the partition. RANK says how many rows before the current one, and DENSE_RANK says how many different values come before the current value. Another way to think about this is that DENSE_RANK doesn't waste any numbers, while RANK skips numbers.

The syntax of these two functions looks a lot like the syntax of ROW_NUMBER:

```
RANK() OVER([PARTITION BY <col1>[,<col2>,...<n>]] ORDER BY <col3>[,<col4>])
DENSE_RANK() OVER([PARTITION BY <col1>[,<col2>,...<n>]]
ORDER BY <col3>[,<col4>])
```

Listing 2-4 compares ROW_NUMBER to RANK and DENSE_RANK.

Listing 2-4. Using RANK and DENSE_RANK

```
--2-4.1 Using RANK and DENSE_RANK
SELECT CustomerID, OrderDate,
    ROW_NUMBER() OVER(ORDER BY OrderDate) AS RowNumber,
    RANK() OVER(ORDER BY OrderDate) AS [Rank],
    DENSE_RANK() OVER(ORDER BY OrderDate) AS DenseRank
FROM Sales.SalesOrderHeader
WHERE CustomerID IN (11330, 29676);
```

Figure 2-4 shows the partial results. The query has been filtered to return two customers who have placed multiple orders on the same date, and the ORDER BY column in each OVER clause is OrderDate. The row numbers are unique and sequential, just as expected. Notice that the Rank values of the third and fourth row are both 3. Both of those rows have the OrderDate of 2013-07-31, a tie. This is the third highest OrderDate in the set of rows. On row 5, the Rank "catches up" with the RowNumber value, 5. The date 2013-08-09 in the fifth row is the fifth highest OrderDate in the set.

	CustomerID	OrderDate	RowNumber	Rank	DenseRank
1	11330	2013-07-15 00:00:00.000	1	1	1
2	11330	2013-07-26 00:00:00.000	2	2	2
3	29676	2013-07-31 00:00:00.000	3	3	3
4	29676	2013-07-31 00:00:00.000	4	3	3
5	11330	2013-08-09 00:00:00.000	5	5	4
6	11330	2013-10-11 00:00:00.000	6	6	5
7	11330	2013-10-16 00:00:00.000	7	7	6
8	11330	2013-10-24 00:00:00.000	8	8	7

Figure 2-4. *Partial results comparing ROW_NUMBER, RANK, and DENSE_RANK*

The DenseRank values for rows 3 and 4 are also both 3. Notice that the DenseRank for row 5 is 4, however. The date 2013-08-09 is the fourth highest *distinct* OrderDate in the set.

The ROW_NUMBER, RANK, and DENSE_RANK functions assign a number to each row. Now you will learn about a different type of ranking function, NTILE.

Dividing Data with NTILE

The NTILE function is considered to be a ranking function, but with a twist. The numbers applied are used to divide the results into equal buckets. You must specify how many buckets are needed and an ORDER BY expression is required in the OVER clause. Here is the syntax for NTILE:

```
NTILE(<buckets>) OVER([PARTITION BY <col1>[,<col2>,...<n>]]
ORDER BY <col3>[,<col4>])
```

Within the parentheses after the word NTILE, supply the number of buckets. The PARTITION BY is optional, and the ORDER BY is required. Listing 2-5 shows an example that divides the months into four buckets depending on the sales of 2013.

Listing 2-5. Using NTILE

```
--2.5.1 Using NTILE
WITH Orders AS (
    SELECT MONTH(OrderDate) AS OrderMonth,
        FORMAT(SUM(TotalDue),'C') AS Sales
    FROM Sales.SalesOrderHeader
    WHERE OrderDate >= '2013/01/01' and OrderDate < '2014/01/01'
        GROUP BY MONTH(OrderDate))
SELECT OrderMonth, Sales, NTILE(4) OVER(ORDER BY Sales) AS Bucket
FROM Orders;
```

Figure 2-5 shows the results. The query aggregates the sales from 2013 into months inside a CTE called Orders. In the outer query, the NTILE function is applied. The bucket that each month falls into depends on the sales for that month. Bucket #1 contains the three months with the lowest sales. Bucket #4 contains the three months with the highest sales.

	OrderMonth	Sales	Bucket
1	1	$2,340,061.55	1
2	2	$2,600,218.87	1
3	4	$2,840,711.17	1
4	5	$3,658,084.95	2
5	11	$3,694,668.00	2
6	8	$3,733,973.00	2
7	3	$3,831,605.94	3
8	12	$4,560,577.10	3
9	9	$5,083,505.34	3
10	10	$5,374,375.94	4
11	7	$5,521,840.84	4
12	6	$5,726,265.26	4

Figure 2-5. *Using NTILE*

In this example, using four buckets, the data divided up evenly into the buckets. Sometimes the rows are not evenly divided by the bucket number. When there is one extra row after dividing, bucket #1 will get an extra row. When there are two extra rows after dividing, buckets #1 and #2 will get an extra row. Listing 2-6 demonstrates this.

Listing 2-6. Using NTILE with Uneven Buckets

```
--2.6.1 Using NTILE with uneven buckets
WITH Orders AS (
    SELECT MONTH(OrderDate) AS OrderMonth, FORMAT(SUM(TotalDue),'C')
        AS Sales
    FROM Sales.SalesOrderHeader
    WHERE OrderDate >= '2013/01/01' and OrderDate < '2014/01/01'
    GROUP BY MONTH(OrderDate))
SELECT OrderMonth, Sales, NTILE(5) OVER(ORDER BY Sales) AS Bucket
FROM Orders;
```

This query returns five buckets. Twelve divided by five is two with a remainder of two. If you take a look at the results shown in Figure 2-6, you will see that buckets #1 and #2 each have an extra row. The other buckets each have two rows.

	OrderMonth	Sales	Bucket
1	1	$2,340,061.55	1
2	2	$2,600,218.87	1
3	4	$2,840,711.17	1
4	5	$3,658,084.95	2
5	11	$3,694,668.00	2
6	8	$3,733,973.00	2
7	3	$3,831,605.94	3
8	12	$4,560,577.10	3
9	9	$5,083,505.34	4
10	10	$5,374,375.94	4
11	7	$5,521,840.84	5
12	6	$5,726,265.26	5

Figure 2-6. *The results of NTILE with uneven buckets*

You have seen many examples explaining how to use the ranking functions in this chapter, but you have not seen many practical examples. The next section will demonstrate some real-world problems that can be solved with these functions.

Solving Queries with Ranking Functions

Over the past ten years, I have found more and more reasons to use the ranking functions when writing queries. I believe they have helped me learn to think in a set-based manner. When I am faced with a challenging query, I often just add a row number to see if I can find any patterns.

Deduplicating Data

There is always more than one way to solve a problem, and deduplicating data is a good example. The traditional approach involves storing the distinct rows in a temp table. Then you can truncate the original table and insert the rows back in from the temp table. There could be a situation in which you cannot empty the original table, and must selectively delete the extra rows. You can solve this problem using a row number. Listing 2-7 creates a table with duplicate rows.

Listing 2-7. Creating a Table with Duplicate Rows

```
--2-7.1 Create a table that will hold duplicate rows
CREATE TABLE #dupes(Col1 INT, Col2 CHAR(1));

--2-7.2 Insert some rows
INSERT INTO #dupes(Col1, Col2)
VALUES (1,'a'),(1,'a'),(2,'b'),
    (3,'c'),(4,'d'),(4,'d'),(5,'e');

--2-7.3
SELECT Col1, Col2
FROM #dupes;
```

Figure 2-7 shows the results. You can see that several rows are duplicates.

	Col1	Col2
1	1	a
2	1	a
3	2	b
4	3	c
5	4	d
6	4	d
7	5	e

Figure 2-7. *The table with duplicate rows*

Listing 2-8 contains a script to remove the duplicates. To better understand how this works, it is broken down into several steps. Be sure to run this code in the same query window as Listing 2-7 so that the temp table is in place.

Listing 2-8. Removing the Duplicate Rows

```
--2-8.1 Add ROW_NUMBER and Partition by all of the columns
SELECT Col1, Col2,
    ROW_NUMBER() OVER(PARTITION BY Col1, Col2 ORDER BY Col1) AS RowNumber
FROM #dupes;

--2-8.2 Delete the rows with RowNumber > 1
WITH Dupes AS (
    SELECT Col1, Col2,
        ROW_NUMBER() OVER(PARTITION BY Col1, Col2 ORDER BY Col1)
            AS RowNumber
    FROM #dupes)
DELETE Dupes WHERE RowNumber > 1;

--2-8.3 The results
SELECT Col1, Col2
FROM #dupes;
```

Figure 2-8 shows the results of running this script. A ROW_NUMBER function is added to Query 1. To get the row numbers to start over for each unique row, partition by all of the columns in the table. This table has only two columns, but if it had more, they would all be listed in the PARTITION BY expression. Since the row numbers start over for each unique row, it is easy to see the rows to delete: they all have row numbers greater than 1. Statement 2 deletes those rows. Because you cannot add the ROW_NUMBER function to the WHERE clause, the logic is separated by adding the row number in a CTE. The duplicates are deleted directly from the CTE. Finally, Query 3 demonstrates that the duplicates are gone.

	Col1	Col2	RowNumber
1	1	a	1
2	1	a	2
3	2	b	1
4	3	c	1
5	4	d	1
6	4	d	2
7	5	e	1

	Col1	Col2
1	1	a
2	2	b
3	3	c
4	4	d
5	5	e

Figure 2-8. *Removing duplicate rows*

Finding the First N Rows of Every Group

I first thought about this problem during a technical interview. The potential customer wanted to know how I would find the first four orders of every month within a particular year. One method of solving it involves using CROSS APPLY and TOP. The solution that is easiest to write uses ROW_NUMBER. Listing 2-9 shows both methods.

Listing 2-9. Finding the First Four Orders of Each Month

```
--2-9.1 Using CROSS APPLY to find the first four orders
WITH Months AS (
    SELECT MONTH(OrderDate) AS OrderMonth
    FROM Sales.SalesOrderHeader
    WHERE OrderDate >= '2013-01-01' AND OrderDate < '2014-01-01'
    GROUP BY MONTH(OrderDate))
SELECT OrderMonth, CA.OrderDate, CA.SalesOrderID, CA.TotalDue
FROM Months
```

```
CROSS APPLY (
    SELECT TOP(4) SalesOrderID, OrderDate, TotalDue
    FROM Sales.SalesOrderHeader AS IQ
    WHERE OrderDate >= '2013-01-01' AND OrderDate < '2014-01-01'
        AND MONTH(IQ.OrderDate) =MONTHS.OrderMonth
    ORDER BY SalesOrderID) AS CA
ORDER BY OrderMonth, SalesOrderID;

--2-9.2 Use ROW_NUMBER to find the first four orders
WITH Orders AS (
    SELECT  MONTH(OrderDate) AS OrderMonth, OrderDate,
        SalesOrderID, TotalDue,
        ROW_NUMBER() OVER(PARTITION BY MONTH(OrderDate)
            ORDER BY SalesOrderID) AS RowNumber
    FROM Sales.SalesOrderHeader
    WHERE OrderDate >= '2013-01-01' AND OrderDate < '2014-01-01')
SELECT OrderMonth, OrderDate, SalesOrderID, TotalDue
FROM Orders
WHERE RowNumber <= 4
ORDER BY OrderMonth, SalesOrderID;
```

Figure 2-9 shows the partial results, the rows for January and February. Query 1 is complex. In my opinion, it is not easy to figure out. The CTE creates a list of months for sales year 2013. The outer query joins the Months CTE to an inner query using CROSS APPLY. In order to pull back the first four rows for each row of the outer query, TOP is used. CROSS APPLY must be used in this case because using a derived table will just pull back a total of four rows, not four rows for each month.

	OrderMonth	OrderDate	SalesOrderID	TotalDue
1	1	2013-01-01 00:00:00.000	49181	2410.6266
2	1	2013-01-01 00:00:00.000	49182	2699.9018
3	1	2013-01-01 00:00:00.000	49183	2699.9018
4	1	2013-01-01 00:00:00.000	49184	2264.2536
5	2	2013-02-01 00:00:00.000	49581	2699.9018
6	2	2013-02-01 00:00:00.000	49582	2410.6266
7	2	2013-02-01 00:00:00.000	49583	2410.6266
8	2	2013-02-01 00:00:00.000	49584	2699.9018

	OrderMonth	OrderDate	SalesOrderID	TotalDue
1	1	2013-01-01 00:00:00.000	49181	2410.6266
2	1	2013-01-01 00:00:00.000	49182	2699.9018
3	1	2013-01-01 00:00:00.000	49183	2699.9018
4	1	2013-01-01 00:00:00.000	49184	2264.2536
5	2	2013-02-01 00:00:00.000	49581	2699.9018
6	2	2013-02-01 00:00:00.000	49582	2410.6266
7	2	2013-02-01 00:00:00.000	49583	2410.6266
8	2	2013-02-01 00:00:00.000	49584	2699.9018

Figure 2-9. Partial results of returning the first four sales of each month

Query 2 uses ROW_NUMBER to accomplish the same thing. The CTE contains all of the expressions needed in the results plus a row number. The row number is partitioned by month, so that the numbers start over for each month. The outer query simply retrieves the data from the CTE and filters on the row number.

Solving the Islands Problem

The islands-and-gaps problem is a classic. Imagine that you have sequential ID numbers in your data, and some of those ID numbers are missing. Your job is to find the groups of ID numbers without gaps. Those are the islands. You can use the one of the ranking functions to solve this problem. You will learn how to find the gaps, the missing numbers, in Chapter 7.

Take a look at this series of numbers: 101, 102, 103, 106, 108, 108, 109, 110, 111, 112, 112, 114, 115, 118, and 119. The islands in the series are 101-103, 106, 108-112, 114-115, and 118-119. Listing 2-10 creates a table and populates it with these values.

Listing 2-10. Creating the Table with Islands

```
--2-10.1 Create the #Islands table
CREATE TABLE #Islands(ID INT NOT NULL ) ;

--2-10.2 Populate the #Islands table
INSERT INTO #Islands(ID)
VALUES(101),(102),(103),(106),(108),(108),(109),(110),(111),(112),(112),
    (114),(115),(118),(119);

--2-10.3 View the data
SELECT ID
FROM #Islands;
```

Because this data has duplicates in the ID column, the solution uses the DENSE_RANK function. If the values were unique, you could use ROW_NUMBER. Listing 2-11 has the solution.

Listing 2-11. The Solution to the Islands Problem

```
--2-11.1 Add ROW_NUMBER to the data
SELECT ID, ROW_NUMBER() OVER(ORDER BY ID) AS RowNum
FROM #Islands;

--2-11.2 Subtract the RowNum from the ID
SELECT ID, ROW_NUMBER() OVER(ORDER BY ID) AS RowNum,
    ID - ROW_NUMBER() OVER(ORDER BY ID) AS Diff
FROM #Islands;

--2-11.3 Change to DENSE_RANK since there are duplicates
SELECT ID, DENSE_RANK() OVER(ORDER BY ID) AS DenseRank,
    ID - DENSE_RANK() OVER(ORDER BY ID) AS Diff
FROM #Islands;

--2-11.4 The complete Islands solution
WITH Islands AS (
    SELECT ID, DENSE_RANK() OVER(ORDER BY ID) AS DenseRank,
        ID - DENSE_RANK() OVER(ORDER BY ID) AS Diff
    FROM #Islands)
SELECT MIN(ID) AS IslandStart, MAX(ID) AS IslandEnd
FROM Islands
GROUP BY Diff;
```

To save space, Figure 2-10 contains just the results of the complete solution found in Query 4. Query 1 adds a row number to the data. If you look at the results of this query, you will see a pattern beginning to emerge. The difference between the numbers of the first island and the row number is 100. The second island, just the number 106, has a difference of 101 from the row number. Query 2 adds an expression that subtracts the row number from the value to take advantage of this pattern.

	IslandStart	IslandEnd
1	101	103
2	106	106
3	108	112
4	114	115
5	118	119

Figure 2-10. *The islands*

If you look a bit further, you will see a problem. There are two rows with value 108. One has a difference of 103 and one has a difference of 102. Instead of using ROW_NUMBER, switch to DENSE_RANK as in Query 3. The RANK function will not work because the numbers revert back to the ROW_NUMBER values after a tie. You need an ever increasing difference here, so DENSE_RANK is the correct choice.

The final step is to group on the difference. Since you cannot group on a window function, the entire solution so far is placed in a CTE in Query 4. The outer query groups by the difference. Then, by using the MIN and MAX functions, the islands in the data are found.

Solving the Bonus Problem

This example is one that I have used over the years to explain how to use the NTILE function. Imagine that you are a manager with a team of salespeople. You have bonus money to give out and want to divide the money based on how much each person has sold. Listing 2-12 shows how to solve this problem using NTILE.

Listing 2-12. Solving the Bonus Problem

```
--2-12.1 Using NTILE to assign bonuses
WITH Sales AS (
    SELECT SP.FirstName, SP.LastName,
        SUM(SOH.TotalDue) AS TotalSales
    FROM [Sales].[vSalesPerson] SP
    JOIN Sales.SalesOrderHeader SOH
            ON SP.BusinessEntityID = SOH.SalesPersonID
    WHERE SOH.OrderDate >= '2011-01-01' AND SOH.OrderDate < '2012-01-01'
    GROUP BY FirstName, LastName)
SELECT FirstName, LastName, TotalSales,
    NTILE(4) OVER(ORDER BY TotalSales) * 1000 AS Bonus
FROM Sales;
```

Figure 2-11 shows the results. This query filters for just one year, 2011. The data is aggregated, and sum of TotalSales is calculated for each person inside a CTE called Sales. In the outer query, the NTILE function divides the rows into four buckets. By multiplying the bucket number by 1000, the bonus is returned. The salespeople with the lowest sales get the smaller bonus.

	FirstName	LastName	TotalSales	Bonus
1	Stephen	Jiang	32567.9155	1000
2	Garrett	Vargas	563326.5478	1000
3	David	Campbell	675663.694	1000
4	Pamela	Ansman-Wolfe	730273.4889	2000
5	Michael	Blythe	986298.0902	2000
6	Shu	Ito	1089874.3906	2000
7	Linda	Mitchell	1294819.7439	3000
8	José	Saraiva	1323328.6346	3000
9	Jillian	Carson	1477158.2811	4000
10	Tsvi	Reiter	1713640.8372	4000

Figure 2-11. The results of the bonus problem

Summary

The ranking functions, ROW_NUMBER, RANK, DENSE_RANK, NTILE, are the most basic of all the window functions. The ranking functions add a number to each row of the results. The ORDER BY expression of the OVER clause is required, and, depending on the situation, you may also want to add PARTITION BY. These functions are usually not the solution in themselves, but often form the basis of a more complex solution.

When faced with a tricky query, you may want to add a row number to look for patterns or relationships between the rows. Then use those patterns and relationships to figure out the solution.

Chapter 3 covers window aggregates, which allow you to add functions like SUM or AVG to a query without turning the query into an aggregate query. You won't need GROUP BY, and you won't lose any detail.

CHAPTER 3

■ ■ ■

Summarizing with Window Aggregates

One big difference between using window functions and aggregate queries is that you lose the details with aggregate queries. Starting with SQL Server 2005, you can eliminate that restriction by adding the OVER clause. By adding OVER, you may also eliminate the GROUP BY and HAVING clauses.

In this chapter, you will learn how to use window aggregate functions to easily add aggregate functions to non-aggregate queries. You will finish up the chapter by taking a look at some real-world problems.

Using Window Aggregates

Window aggregates are those favorite aggregate functions that you use every day, like SUM and AVG, with the addition of the OVER clause. So far you have seen the OVER clause used with LAG and the ranking functions. In those situations, an ORDER BY component is required. The ORDER BY component *is not supported* with SQL Server 2005's window aggregate functionality. Chapter 5 covers a 2012 enhancement that does use ORDER BY, but you must learn about the 2005 feature first.

Although the ORDER BY component is not supported in the OVER clause, all window functions support PARTITION BY, and window aggregates are no exception. When leaving out PARTITION BY, you will have an empty OVER clause, and the function is applied to the entire set of results, for example, a grand total. When including PARTITION BY, the function is applied to the individual partitions, for example, subtotals. Here is the syntax:

```
<AggregateFunction>(<col1>) OVER([PARTITION BY <col2>[,<col3>,...<colN>])
```

The built-in aggregate functions that may be used as a window aggregate are listed in Table 3-1.

Table 3-1. *The List of Window Aggregate Functions*

Aggregate Function	Definition
AVG	Calculates the average over the group.
CHECKSUM_AGG	Calculates the checksum over the group. This is often used to detect changes in the data.
COUNT	Used to get a count of the rows or a count of non-null values of a column.
COUNT_BIG	Works like COUNT, but returns a big integer.
MAX	Returns the highest value in the set.
MIN	Returns the lowest value in the set.
STDEV	Calculates the standard deviation over the group.
STDEVP	Calculates the standard deviation for the population over the group.
SUM	Adds up the values over the group.
VAR	Returns the statistical variance over the group.
VARP	Returns the statistical variance for the population over the group.

The examples in this chapter will focus on the commonly used functions AVG, SUM, MIN, MAX, and COUNT. Listing 3-1 shows some examples of window aggregates.

Listing 3-1. Using Window Aggregates

```
--3.1.1 Window aggregate examples
SELECT CustomerID, SalesOrderID,
    FORMAT(MIN(OrderDate) OVER(),'yyyy-MM-dd') AS FirstOrderDate,
    FORMAT(MAX(OrderDate) OVER(),'yyyy-MM-dd') AS LastOrderDate,
    COUNT(*) OVER() OrderCount,
    FORMAT(SUM(TotalDue) OVER(),'C') TotalAmount
FROM Sales.SalesOrderHeader
ORDER BY CustomerID, SalesOrderID;

--3.1.2 Use PARTITION BY
SELECT CustomerID, SalesOrderID,
    FORMAT(MIN(OrderDate) OVER(PARTITION BY CustomerID),'yyyy-MM-dd')
        AS FirstOrderDate,
    FORMAT(MAX(OrderDate) OVER(PARTITION BY CustomerID) ,'yyyy-MM-dd')
        AS LastOrderDate,
```

```
  COUNT(*) OVER(PARTITION BY CustomerID) OrderCount,
  FORMAT(SUM(TotalDue) OVER(PARTITION BY CustomerID),'C') AS TotalAmount
FROM Sales.SalesOrderHeader
ORDER BY CustomerID, SalesOrderID;
```

Figure 3-1 shows the partial results. The first thing to notice about the examples is that there is no GROUP BY clause in either of the queries. Adding a window aggregate expression to an otherwise non-aggregate query does not change the query to an aggregate query. These queries show details of each row along with summary values. Another thing to notice is that the window aggregate functions are nested inside the FORMAT function. The window functions may also operate on columns, more complex expressions, or subqueries just like regular aggregate functions. If you are not familiar with the FORMAT function, it was added with SQL Server 2012 along with several other functions I like to call the "easy functions."

	CustomerID	SalesOrderID	FirstOrderDate	LastOrderDate	OrderCount	TotalAmount
1	11000	43793	2011-05-31	2014-06-30	31465	$123,216,786.12
2	11000	51522	2011-05-31	2014-06-30	31465	$123,216,786.12
3	11000	57418	2011-05-31	2014-06-30	31465	$123,216,786.12
4	11001	43767	2011-05-31	2014-06-30	31465	$123,216,786.12
5	11001	51493	2011-05-31	2014-06-30	31465	$123,216,786.12
6	11001	72773	2011-05-31	2014-06-30	31465	$123,216,786.12

	CustomerID	SalesOrderID	FirstOrderDate	LastOrderDate	OrderCount	TotalAmount
1	11000	43793	2011-06-21	2013-10-03	3	$9,115.13
2	11000	51522	2011-06-21	2013-10-03	3	$9,115.13
3	11000	57418	2011-06-21	2013-10-03	3	$9,115.13
4	11001	43767	2011-06-17	2014-05-12	3	$7,054.19
5	11001	51493	2011-06-17	2014-05-12	3	$7,054.19
6	11001	72773	2011-06-17	2014-05-12	3	$7,054.19

Figure 3-1. *Partial results of using window aggregates*

Query 1 uses the empty OVER clause. This means that the calculation is performed over the entire set of results. The FirstOrderDate is the earliest OrderDate in the data. The TotalAmount is the grand total of all rows. Query 2 includes a PARTITION BY on CustomerID in each OVER clause. Notice in the results that the values for Query 2 are specific for each customer.

In the previous example, the OVER clause was identical within each query. You may have different OVER clauses within a query. Listing 3-2 has two window functions with different OVER clauses.

Listing 3-2. Using Different OVER Clauses

```
--3.2.1 Use different OVER clauses
SELECT CustomerID, SalesOrderID, FORMAT(TotalDue,'c') AS TotalDue,
    FORMAT(SUM(TotalDue) OVER(PARTITION BY CustomerID),'c')
    AS CustomerSales,
    FORMAT(SUM(TotalDue) OVER(),'c') AS TotalSales
FROM Sales.SalesOrderHeader
WHERE OrderDate >= '2013-01-01' AND OrderDate < '2014-01-01'
ORDER BY CustomerID, SalesOrderID;
```

Figure 3-2 shows the partial results. This query returns the total for each customer and the overall total. Notice that the window aggregates are nested in another function.

	CustomerID	SalesOrderID	TotalDue	CustomerSales	TotalSales
1	11000	51522	$2,587.88	$5,358.15	$48,965,887.96
2	11000	57418	$2,770.27	$5,358.15	$48,965,887.96
3	11001	51493	$2,674.02	$2,674.02	$48,965,887.96
4	11002	51238	$2,535.96	$5,209.03	$48,965,887.96
5	11002	53237	$2,673.06	$5,209.03	$48,965,887.96
6	11003	51315	$2,562.45	$5,236.93	$48,965,887.96

Figure 3-2. *The partial results of using different OVER clauses*

You can see that it is easy to add a window aggregate function to any non-aggregate query. Follow the rules on data types; for example, you can't calculate a sum on character data. The PARTITION BY expression, if needed, can be a column, a more complex expression, or even a subquery.

A very nonintuitive use of window aggregates is using them within an aggregate query.

Adding Window Aggregates to Aggregate Queries

The first time I added a window aggregate to an aggregate query, I was surprised that it didn't work and more surprised at the error message. Listing 3-3 shows an example.

Listing 3-3. Adding a Window Aggregate to an Aggregate Query

```
--3-3.1 Add a window aggregate to an aggregate query
SELECT CustomerID, SUM(TotalDue) AS CustomerTotal,
    SUM(TotalDue) OVER() AS GrandTotal
FROM Sales.SalesOrderHeader
GROUP BY CustomerID;
```

Figure 3-3 shows the error message.

```
Messages
Msg 8120, Level 16, State 1, Line 2
Column 'Sales.SalesOrderHeader.TotalDue' is invalid
in the select list because it is not contained in either
an aggregate function or the GROUP BY clause.
```

Figure 3-3. *The error message from adding a window aggregate to an aggregate query*

Obviously, the TotalDue column *is contained* in an aggregate expression, and adding it to the GROUP BY is certainly not the solution. To understand what is going on here, you have to think about the window that the window aggregate is operating on. The set of rows in the window is created from the GROUP BY operation. The window contains any expression listed in the GROUP BY clause plus any aggregate expressions. Any expression contained in any part of a window function must follow the same rules as the SELECT list. This means that adding CustomerID as the operand of the function or as a PARTITION BY is fine because CustomerID is part of the GROUP BY. To use TotalDue in any role of the window aggregate expression, it must be aggregated first. Listing 3-4 shows the correct solution.

Listing 3-4. How to Add a Window Aggregate to an Aggregate Query

```
--3-4.1 How to add a window aggregate to an aggregate query
SELECT CustomerID, SUM(TotalDue) AS CustomerTotal,
    SUM(SUM(TotalDue)) OVER() AS GrandTotal
FROM Sales.SalesOrderHeader
GROUP BY CustomerID;
```

The syntax may look unusual, but the window function must be applied to the sum of TotalDue, not just TotalDue. Figure 3-4 shows the partial results and proves that this works.

	CustomerID	CustomerTotal	GrandTotal
1	14324	5659.1783	123216786.1159
2	22814	5.514	123216786.1159
3	11407	59.659	123216786.1159
4	28387	645.2869	123216786.1159
5	19897	659.6408	123216786.1159
6	15675	7963.05	123216786.1159
7	24165	3366.7583	123216786.1159
8	27036	8.0444	123216786.1159

Figure 3-4. *Partial results of adding a window aggregate to an aggregate query*

Listing 3-5 is another interesting example involving multiple expressions in the GROUP BY clause.

Listing 3-5. Adding a Window Aggregate to a Query with Multiple Expressions in the GROUP BY Clause

```
--3-5.1 Window aggregate to multiple group by
SELECT YEAR(OrderDate) AS OrderYear,
    CustomerID, SUM(TotalDue) AS CustTotalForYear,
    SUM(SUM(TotalDue)) OVER(PARTITION BY CustomerID) AS CustomerTotal
FROM Sales.SalesOrderHeader
GROUP BY CustomerID, YEAR(OrderDate)
ORDER BY CustomerID, OrderYear;
```

The partial results are shown in Figure 3-5. The GROUP BY clause lists the column CustomerID and the expression YEAR(OrderDate). The default window contains one row for each customer per year. The partition could be the entire set of results, partitioned by CustomerID, or partitioned by YEAR(OrderYear).

	OrderYear	CustomerID	CustTotalForYear	CustomerTotal
1	2011	11000	3756.989	9115.1341
2	2013	11000	5358.1451	9115.1341
3	2011	11001	3729.364	7054.1875
4	2013	11001	2674.0227	7054.1875
5	2014	11001	650.8008	7054.1875
6	2011	11002	3756.989	8966.0143
7	2013	11002	5209.0253	8966.0143
8	2011	11003	3756.989	8993.9155

Figure 3-5. Using a window aggregate with multiple GROUP BY expressions

You start out with the filtered rows. After grouping, the list of columns available is restricted by the GROUP BY. This is the default window; you can partition it, but you cannot include anything outside it.

The rules for adding a window aggregate to an aggregate query apply to all of the window functions. Always keep in mind that the GROUP BY and HAVING clauses operate first. The results of the FROM, WHERE, GROUP BY, and HAVING clauses determine the rows and columns in the base window and the granularity. Any column used anywhere in the window function must be one of the GROUP BY columns or aggregated inside the window function.

There is another way around this. Do the first aggregation in a CTE. Then, in the outer query, apply the window function.

Using Window Aggregates to Solve Common Queries

It is very easy to add a window aggregate to a complex non-aggregated query. To do the same thing with other methods could double the size of the query.

The Percent of Sales Problem

This particular example can be applied to many situations. You can perform a calculation, such as a percentage, using a window aggregate. Listing 3-6 demonstrates how to display the details along with a percent of sales.

Listing 3-6. Using a Window Function to Display Percent of Sales

```
--3-6.1 Calculate the percent of sales
SELECT P.ProductID,
    FORMAT(SUM(OrderQty * UnitPrice),'C') AS ProductSales,
    FORMAT(SUM(SUM(OrderQty * UnitPrice)) OVER(),'C') AS TotalSales,
    FORMAT(SUM(OrderQty * UnitPrice)/
        SUM(SUM(OrderQty * UnitPrice)) OVER(), 'P') AS PercentOfSales
FROM Sales.SalesOrderDetail AS SOD
JOIN Production.Product AS P ON SOD.ProductID = P.ProductID
JOIN Production.ProductSubcategory AS SUB ON P.ProductSubcategoryID
    = SUB.ProductSubcategoryID
JOIN Production.ProductCategory AS CAT ON SUB.ProductCategoryID
    = CAT.ProductCategoryID
WHERE CAT.Name = 'Bikes'
GROUP BY P.ProductID
ORDER BY PercentOfSales DESC;
```

Figure 3-6 shows the partial results. This is an aggregate query, so the columns used in any role inside the window aggregate must be a GROUP BY column or aggregated. The empty OVER clause is used to calculate TotalSales. The sum by ProductID is divided by the sales over the entire result set and formatted to give the percentage of sales for each bike model.

	ProductID	ProductSales	TotalSales	PercentOfSales
1	782	$4,406,151.27	$95,145,813.35	4.63 %
2	783	$4,014,067.80	$95,145,813.35	4.21 %
3	779	$3,696,486.47	$95,145,813.35	3.88 %
4	780	$3,441,292.54	$95,145,813.35	3.61 %
5	781	$3,436,090.79	$95,145,813.35	3.61 %
6	784	$3,311,098.44	$95,145,813.35	3.48 %
7	793	$2,518,299.76	$95,145,813.35	2.64 %
8	794	$2,348,246.09	$95,145,813.35	2.46 %

Figure 3-6. The percent of sales by ProductID

The Partitioned Table Problem

One of my favorite examples involves looking at the metadata of table partitions. Table partitions have nothing to do with PARTITION BY, it's an Enterprise-level feature that makes data management easier. Since no tables in the AdventureWorks database are partitioned, run Listing 3-7 to create a partitioned table. You must have either the Enterprise or Developer Edition to run this script.

Listing 3-7. Creating a Partitioned Table

```
--3-7.1 Create the partition function
CREATE PARTITION FUNCTION testFunction (DATE)
AS RANGE RIGHT
FOR VALUES ('2011-01-01','2012-01-01','2013-01-01','2014-01-01');
GO


--3-7.2 Create the partition scheme
CREATE PARTITION SCHEME testScheme
AS PARTITION testFunction ALL TO ('Primary');
GO


--3-7.3 Create a partitioned table
CREATE TABLE dbo.Orders(CustomerID INT, SalesOrderID INT,
    OrderDate DATE, TotalDue MONEY)
ON testScheme(OrderDate);
GO


--3-7.4 Populate the table
INSERT INTO dbo.Orders(customerID, SalesOrderID,
    OrderDate, TotalDue)
SELECT CustomerID, SalesOrderID,
    OrderDate, TotalDue
FROM Sales.SalesOrderHeader;
GO


--3-7.5 Create another partitioned table
CREATE TABLE dbo.Customer (CustomerID INT, ModifiedDate DATE)
ON testScheme(ModifiedDate);
GO


--3-7.6 Populate the table
INSERT INTO dbo.Customer(CustomerID, ModifiedDate)
SELECT CustomerID, ModifiedDate
FROM Sales.Customer;
```

My colleague sent me a query and asked for some help. He wanted to see what percentage of rows was found in each partition per table. Listing 3-8 shows the query and the solution.

Listing 3-8. The Table Partition Question and Solution

```
--3-8.1 Find the percent of rows by table
SELECT OBJECT_NAME(p.OBJECT_ID) TableName,
    ps.partition_number, ps.Row_count,
    --My solution starts here
    FORMAT(ps.row_count * 1.0 /
        SUM(ps.row_count) OVER(PARTITION BY p.OBJECT_ID),'p')
        As PercentOfRows
    --and ends here
FROM sys.data_spaces  d
JOIN sys.indexes i
JOIN (SELECT DISTINCT OBJECT_ID
    FROM sys.partitions
    WHERE partition_number > 1) p
ON i.OBJECT_ID = p.OBJECT_ID
ON d.data_space_id = i.data_space_id
JOIN sys.dm_db_partition_stats ps
ON i.OBJECT_ID = ps.OBJECT_ID and i.index_id = ps.index_id
WHERE i.index_id < 2;
```

Figure 3-7 shows the results. The original query sent to me contained all of the columns in the results except for the PercentOfRows column. Hopefully, you agree that the original query is complex. To get the desired solution, the Row_count column is divided by the sum of the Row_count partitioned by OBJECT_ID, which is specific to each table. The answer is also multiplied by 1.0 to eliminate integer division. It has also been formatted for readability. To accomplish the same thing using older methods would be more difficult to write.

	TableName	partition_number	Row_count	PercentOfRows
1	Orders	1	0	0.00 %
2	Orders	2	1607	5.11 %
3	Orders	3	3915	12.44 %
4	Orders	4	14182	45.07 %
5	Orders	5	11761	37.38 %
6	Customer	1	0	0.00 %
7	Customer	2	0	0.00 %
8	Customer	3	0	0.00 %
9	Customer	4	0	0.00 %
10	Customer	5	19820	100.00 %

Figure 3-7. *The solution to the table partition problem*

To clean up the database objects created in this section, run Listing 3-9.

Listing 3-9. Cleaning Up Database Objects

```
--3-9 Drop objects created in this section
DROP TABLE dbo.Customer;
DROP TABLE dbo.Orders;
DROP PARTITION SCHEME testScheme;
DROP PARTITION FUNCTION testFunction;
```

Whenever you need to use one of the aggregate functions to summarize at a different level than the query's results, think about using a window aggregate.

Creating Custom Window Aggregate Functions

Starting with SQL Server 2005, you can create custom aggregate functions with a .NET language using CLR (Common Language Runtime) integration. Surprisingly, these functions also work as window aggregate functions. Creating a C# DLL is beyond the scope of this book, but the code download for this chapter includes a C# program for such a function. If you would like to learn how to create your own custom function, you can use this project as a model. For more information on creating the custom aggregates, read this MSDN article: http://msdn.microsoft.com/en-us/library/91e6taax(v=vs.90).aspx.

The project contains a DLL file in the chapter's code folder. Copy this file to a location that SQL Server can see. I have created a folder for the project in the C:\ drive. You will need to modify the command in Listing 3-10 if you have copied the file to a different location. CLR integration must be enabled as well, so be sure to do this on a local instance of SQL Server, or at least an instance where you are allowed to change this setting. Run Listing 3-10 to set up the custom window aggregate function.

Listing 3-10. Setting Up a Custom Window Aggregate Function

```
--3-10.1 Enable CRL
EXEC sp_configure 'clr_enabled', 1;
GO
RECONFIGURE;
GO

--3-10.2 Register the DLL
CREATE ASSEMBLY CustomAggregate FROM
 'C:\Custom\CustomAggregate.dll' WITH PERMISSION_SET = SAFE;
GO

--3-10.3 Create the function
CREATE Aggregate Median (@Value INT) RETURNS INT
EXTERNAL NAME CustomAggregate.Median;
GO
```

```
--3-10.4 Test the function
WITH Orders AS (
    SELECT CustomerID, SUM(OrderQty) AS OrderQty, SOH.SalesOrderID
    FROM Sales.SalesOrderHeader AS SOH
    JOIN Sales.SalesOrderDetail AS SOD
        ON SOH.SalesOrderID = SOD.SalesOrderDetailID
    GROUP BY CustomerID, SOH.SalesOrderID)
SELECT CustomerID, OrderQty, dbo.Median(OrderQty) OVER(PARTITION BY
CustomerID) AS Median
FROM Orders
WHERE CustomerID IN (13011, 13012, 13019);
```

Statement 1 turns on CLR integration for the server. Statements 2 and 3 enable the new custom function. Query 4 tests the new function, which is called MEDIAN. Figure 3-8 shows the results of using the MEDIAN function. The median returns the middle value when the number of values is odd. It returns the average of the two middle values when the number of values is even. Customer 13019 has two orders. The median is 6, halfway between 2 and 10.

	CustomerID	OrderQty	Median
1	13011	5	3
2	13011	1	3
3	13011	3	3
4	13012	3	3
5	13012	1	3
6	13012	24	3
7	13019	10	6
8	13019	2	6

Figure 3-8. Using the MEDIAN function

If you wish to remove the function and turn off CLR integration, run Listing 3-11.

Listing 3-11. Cleaning Up the Database

```
--3-11.1 Drop the objects
DROP AGGREGATE Median;
DROP ASSEMBLY CustomAggregate;
GO

--3-11.2 Reset CLR integration to the default
EXEC sp_configure 'clr_enabled', 0;
GO
RECONFIGURE;
```

Summary

Window aggregates make it very easy to add summary calculations to a non-aggregate query. This is very handy when you need to compare the details to an overall total or produce subtotals. While it is easy to use, be sure to pay attention to performance, since it may not always be the best solution. If you are really inspired, you can create your own custom window aggregate function.

You now understand how to use all of the window function features released with SQL Server 2005. Before moving on to the 2012 functionality, Chapter 4 teaches you what you need to know about performance tuning these queries.

CHAPTER 4

■ ■ ■

Tuning for Better Performance

You have learned how to use the window function features of SQL Server 2005: ranking functions and window aggregates. Often, queries using window functions have better performance than using older methods such as self-joins and cursors. There are, however, some things you need to know to make sure your queries run as fast as possible when you use window functions.

In this chapter, you will learn what to look for in execution plans and how to create an index to help any query with a window function.

Using Execution Plans

Graphical execution plans make tuning T-SQL queries easier. You can compare the performance of multiple queries and look for bottlenecks within a query. If graphical execution plans are new to you, you may want to read *SQL Server Performance Tuning* by Grant Fritchey (Apress, 2014) or just follow along and see what you can learn. To turn on the actual execution plans for a query window, type CTRL + M. Be sure that the actual execution plan is toggled on for all examples in this chapter.

There is one execution operator that is specific for window functions; it is the *Sequence Project* operator, which is shown in Figure 4-1. This operator is nothing to worry about. It just means that the column for the computation has been added to the results. You'll see it in the execution plans of many queries with some window functions, but not all. To see the plan, run Listing 4-1.

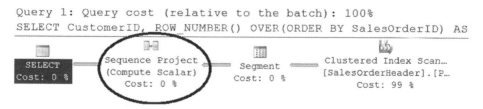

```
Query 1: Query cost (relative to the batch): 100%
SELECT CustomerID, ROW_NUMBER() OVER(ORDER BY SalesOrderID) AS
```

Figure 4-1. A an execution plan with a Sequence Project operator

47

Listing 4-1. Seeing the Sequence Project Operator

```
--4-1.1 Query to produce Sequence Project
SELECT CustomerID, ROW_NUMBER() OVER(ORDER BY SalesOrderID) AS RowNumber
FROM Sales.SalesOrderHeader;
```

Another operator you will see with window function queries is the *Segment* operator, also shown in Figure 4-1 to the right of the Sequence Project operator. The Segment operator divides the input into segments. If there is no PARTITION BY expression, then the segment will be the entire result set. Otherwise, the segments will be divided by the PARTITION BY expressions. Again, the Segment operator is nothing to worry about.

The operator to watch out for, that you can do something about, is the *Sort* operator, shown in Figure 4-2. The Sort operator is found in many types of queries and is often the bottleneck in window function queries. To see the plan, run Listing 4-2.

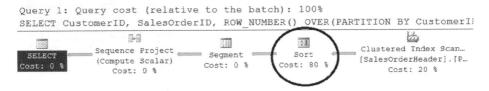

Figure 4-2. *An execution plan with the Sort operator*

Listing 4-2. A Query with a Sort Operator

```
--4-2.1 A query to show the Sort operator
SELECT CustomerID, SalesOrderID,
    ROW_NUMBER() OVER(PARTITION BY CustomerID ORDER BY OrderDate) AS RowNumber
FROM Sales.SalesOrderHeader;
```

Notice that the Sort operator takes 80% of the resources used to run the query. You'll learn how to create an index to eliminate the Sort later in the chapter.

There are two more operators to watch out for. You'll learn more about one of them, the Window Spool operator, in Chapters 5 and 6. For now, take a look at the Table Spool operator shown in Figure 4-3. Run Listing 4-3 to generate the plan yourself.

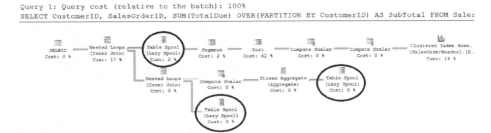

Figure 4-3. *An execution plan with Table Spool operators*

Listing 4-3. A Query Containing Table Spool Operators

```
--4-3.1 A query with a Table Spool operator
SELECT CustomerID, SalesOrderID, SUM(TotalDue)
    OVER(PARTITION BY CustomerID) AS SubTotal
FROM Sales.SalesOrderHeader;
```

The Table Spool operator means that a work table is created in tempdb to help solve the query. You will see Table Spool operators with window aggregates and some other window functions you will learn about in later chapters. This worktable uses a lot of resources, including locks.

Using STATISTICS IO

Another very helpful tool for understanding query performance is STATISTICS IO. This setting will give you information about the pages read to run the query. The nice thing is that it doesn't matter if other queries are running on the server or if the data is already in the cache. If the cache is warm, meaning the needed data is already in memory, the query will often run faster. The logical reads (the number of data pages read) returned will be consistent. That makes it a great tool for comparing two queries or figuring out if a new index has helped. I like to use both the execution plan and STATISTICS IO to make sure I understand what is going on.

Run Listing 4-4 to see how the queries from the previous section compare. While the queries do not produce the same results, it is still interesting to see the difference between them from a performance perspective.

Listing 4-4. Using STATISTICS IO

```
--4.4.0 Settings
SET STATISTICS IO ON;
SET NOCOUNT ON;
GO


--4-4.1 Query to produce Sequence Project
PRINT '4-4.1';
SELECT CustomerID, ROW_NUMBER() OVER(ORDER BY SalesOrderID) AS RowNumber
FROM Sales.SalesOrderHeader;


--4-4.2 A query to show the Sort operator
PRINT '4-4.2';
SELECT CustomerID, SalesOrderID,
    ROW_NUMBER() OVER(PARTITION BY CustomerID ORDER BY OrderDate) AS RowNumber
FROM Sales.SalesOrderHeader;
```

```
--4-4.3 A query with a Table Spool operator
PRINT '4-4.3';
SELECT CustomerID, SalesOrderID, SUM(TotalDue) OVER(PARTITION BY CustomerID)
    AS SubTotal
FROM Sales.SalesOrderHeader;
```

Figure 4-4 shows the results from the Messages tab produced by the STATISTICS IO setting. The listing begins by turning on STATISTICS IO and turning off row counts. Before each query, a PRINT statement prints the query number so that you will know which information goes with which query.

```
4-4.1
Table 'SalesOrderHeader'. Scan count 1, logical reads 689,
4-4.2
Table 'SalesOrderHeader'. Scan count 1, logical reads 689,
4-4.3
Table 'Worktable'. Scan count 3, logical reads 139407, phy
Table 'SalesOrderHeader'. Scan count 1, logical reads 689,
```

Figure 4-4. *The STATISTICS IO ouput from the queries*

The most useful information comes from *logical reads*, which is the number of pages read. Query 1 and Query 2 each take 689 logical reads. That is actually the number of pages in the clustered index of the Sales.SalesOrderHeader table. If you look back at Figure 4-1, you will see that a clustered index scan was performed. Query 3 with a window aggregate takes 689 logical reads to scan the clustered index, but it also creates a worktable in tempdb. It uses 139,407 logical reads to perform the calculations using the worktable.

Using STATISTICS IO can be very beneficial in cases where the execution plans show identical costs, but the queries take a different amount of time to run. I always use both tools when I am tuning queries.

Understanding the Performance Implications of Window Aggregates

Most of the time, using window functions can make your query perform better, especially if your solution eliminates self-joins or cursors. Unfortunately, this is often not the case with the 2005 window aggregate functionality. It sometimes performs worse than other methods. To see the difference, look at the relative cost from the execution plan and the logical reads. Run Listing 4-5 to compare two methods of calculating subtotals.

Listing 4-5. Comparing a Window Aggregate with a CTE

```
--4-5.0 Settings
SET STATISTICS IO ON;
SET NOCOUNT ON;
GO


--4-5.1 CTE
PRINT '4-5.1 CTE';
WITH Totals AS (
    SELECT CustomerID, SUM(TotalDue) AS CustomerTotal
    FROM Sales.SalesOrderHeader
    GROUP BY CustomerID)
SELECT SOH.CustomerID, SalesOrderID, OrderDate, TotalDue, CustomerTotal
FROM Sales.SalesOrderHeader AS SOH
JOIN Totals ON SOH.CustomerID = Totals.CustomerID;

--4-5.1 The same results using a window aggregate
PRINT '4-5.2 The window aggregate';
SELECT CustomerID, SalesOrderID, OrderDate, TotalDue,
    SUM(TotalDue) OVER(PARTITION BY CustomerID) AS CustomerTotal
FROM Sales.SalesOrderHeader;
```

Figure 4-5 shows the STATISTICS IO information from the Messages tab. The CTE method used a total of 1,378 logical reads, which is double the number of pages in the clustered index. The window aggregate method used 689 logical reads to get the data from the table. It then used 139,407 logical reads in a worktable. The CTE method also uses a worktable, but it resides in memory and requires no I/O.

```
4-5.1 CTE
Table 'Workfile'. Scan count 0, logical reads 0, physical r
Table 'Worktable'. Scan count 0, logical reads 0, physical
Table 'SalesOrderHeader'. Scan count 2, logical reads 1378,
4-5.2 The window aggregate
Table 'Worktable'. Scan count 3, logical reads 139407, phys
Table 'SalesOrderHeader'. Scan count 1, logical reads 689,
```

Figure 4-5. *The STATISTICS IO for two methods*

Without digging into the execution plans at this point, notice that the "Query cost (relative to the batch)" for Query 1 is 36% while the relative cost for Query 2 is 64%. Both tools indicate that the CTE method performs better. An interesting thing happens if you sort both queries, for example, by CustomerID and SalesOrderID. The performance of Query 1 drastically decreases so that the logical reads are the same as Query 2, and the execution plans report that the relative costs are also the same.

Does this mean you should never use window aggregates? Of course not, but in situations where you are tuning a query due to performance issues, you may want to use a CTE instead of a window aggregate. One nice thing that does help is that using multiple window aggregate expressions with identical OVER clauses does not add any additional overhead.

Indexing to Improve the Performance of Window Functions

Sorting is often the bottleneck in queries with window functions. You saw the Sort operator take 95% of the resources in the query from Listing 4-2. It is possible, by adding the correct index, to eliminate the sort and decrease the logical reads. The optimum index will sort correctly and cover the query. Of course, you can't add an index for every query you write, but for queries where the performance is critical, you will know what to do.

Rerun the query from Listing 4-2, making sure the Actual Execution Plan setting is toggled on first. Click the Select operator and view the tooltip, as shown in Figure 4-6. You can see a Memory Grant of 4416 reserved as space for sorting and the Estimated Subtree Cost of 2.71698.

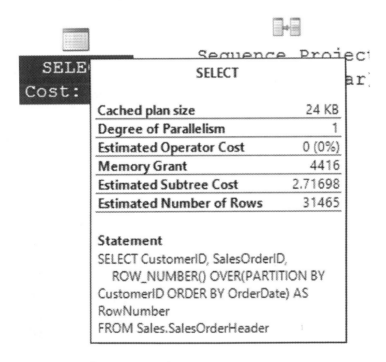

Figure 4-6. *The SELECT tooltip*

Click the Sort operator and then press F4 to see the properties. The Order By property lists two columns. You can more easily see the column names by clicking the ellipsis in the Order By property. Figure 4-7 shows the information.

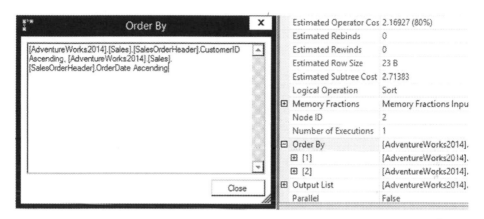

Figure 4-7. *The Order By columns*

The Sort operator is sorting by CustomerID and OrderDate. This makes sense because the PARTITION BY expression is CustomerID and the ORDER BY expression is OrderDate. The data had to be divided by the PARTITION BY column and then sorted by the ORDER BY column. Notice also in the figure that there are three Output List columns. If you dismiss the Order By window and look at the Output List window, you will see CustomerID, OrderDate, and SaleOrderID, the three columns used in the query. The candidate index will have CustomerID and OrderDate as the keys and SalesOrderID as an included column. In this case, SalesOrderID is not required since it is the cluster key of the table and it is already part of any nonclustered index.

Another thing to consider is existing indexes on the table. The table has a nonclustered index on CustomerID, IX_SalesOrderHeader_CustomerID. Instead of creating a new index, you can modify this one. Queries that previously used the old index can now use the new one. Run Listing 4-6 to drop the existing index and create a new one.

Listing 4-6. Modifying the Index

```
--4-6.1 Drop the existing index
DROP INDEX [IX_SalesOrderHeader_CustomerID] ON [Sales].[SalesOrderHeader];
GO

--4-6.2 Create a new index for the query
CREATE NONCLUSTERED INDEX [IX_SalesOrderHeader_CustomerID_OrderDate]
    ON [Sales].[SalesOrderHeader] ([CustomerID], [OrderDate]);
```

Now rerun the query from Listing 4-2. The new execution plan is shown in Figure 4-8.

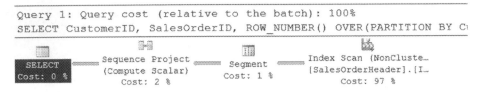

```
Query 1: Query cost (relative to the batch): 100%
SELECT CustomerID, SalesOrderID, ROW_NUMBER() OVER(PARTITION BY C
```

Figure 4-8. The execution plan after the index change

The first thing you should see is that the Sort operator is gone. Now the main cost of running the query is scanning the new nonclustered index. Figure 4-9 shows the SELECT tooltip.

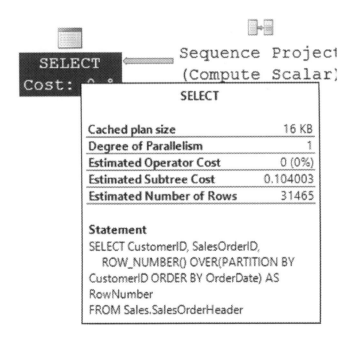

Figure 4-9. The SELECT tooltip after the index change

The Memory Grant is no longer needed, and the Estimated Subtree Cost is just 0.104003. That's quite an improvement! In the case of a query with a WHERE clause, add the column to the index in the first position before the PARTITION BY and OVER columns. In the example above, it would make sense to create a new index instead of adding to the index starting with CustomerID so that existing queries that needed CustomerID as the first key would not be affected.

An index designed this way works well to improve performance by removing the Sort operator for any single table window function query. Most queries, however, have more than one table. Listing 4-7 shows two ways to return the same results from a multi-table query. The queries have different execution plans. The outcome assumes that the index change from Listing 4-6 was made.

Listing 4-7. Window Functions with Joins

```
--4-7.1 query with a join
SELECT SOH.CustomerID, SOH.SalesOrderID, SOH.OrderDate, C.TerritoryID,
    ROW_NUMBER() OVER(PARTITION BY SOH.CustomerID ORDER BY SOH.OrderDate)
        AS RowNumber
FROM Sales.SalesOrderHeader AS SOH
JOIN Sales.Customer C ON SOH.CustomerID = C.CustomerID;

--4-7.2 Rearrange the query
WITH Sales AS (
    SELECT CustomerID, OrderDate, SalesOrderID,
        ROW_NUMBER() OVER(PARTITION BY CustomerID ORDER BY OrderDate)
            AS RowNumber
    FROM Sales.SalesOrderHeader)
SELECT Sales.CustomerID, SALES.SalesOrderID, Sales.OrderDate,
    C.TerritoryID, Sales.RowNumber
FROM Sales
JOIN Sales.Customer AS C ON C.CustomerID = Sales.CustomerID;
```

Figure 4-10 shows the execution plans. Query 1 joins the rows from the Customer and SalesOrderHeader tables with a Merge Join since both indexes are sorted on CustomerID. Then the output is sorted by CustomerID and OrderDate and the row number is calculated. Query 2 moves the SalesOrderHeader table to a CTE and applies the row number there. You can see from the execution plan that the row number is applied before joining to the Customer table. You can also see that the Sort is gone and the relative cost is 12%. In this case, by rearranging the query, the second query performed better. Both the PARTITION BY and ORDER BY columns are from the same query, but that is not always the case. Queries become complex very quickly, and you may not always be able to eliminate sorting. I have seen situations involving queries with several joined tables that had a stubborn Sort operator that I was not able to remove. Fortunately, the cost of sorting was usually small in comparison to other operators in the plan.

```
Query 1: Query cost (relative to the batch): 88%
SELECT SOH.CustomerID, SOH.SalesOrderID, SOH.OrderDate, C.TerritoryID, ROW_NUMBER() OVER(
```

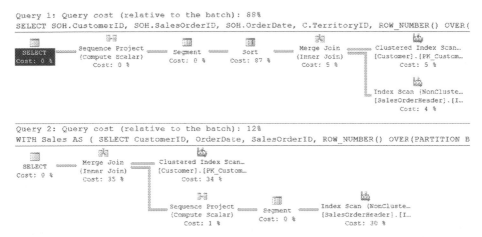

```
Query 2: Query cost (relative to the batch): 12%
WITH Sales AS ( SELECT CustomerID, OrderDate, SalesOrderID, ROW_NUMBER() OVER(PARTITION B
```

Figure 4-10. *The execution plans for a join*

Performing Time Comparisons

So far you have learned what to look for in the execution plan and STATISTICS IO.
You have learned how to create an index to improve performance and why you should
use caution with window aggregates. Your customer, however, will not care about the
execution plan or the logical reads. Your customer only cares about how fast the query
runs. Another setting called STATISTICS TIME can be used to measure how long a query
takes to run. The problem with this information is that it is not consistent. For queries that
run quickly, you really need to run the query multiple times and take an average. Other
workloads on the server can affect the reported time, and whether or not the data is in the
buffer will make a difference as well.

   Another problem I have run into is populating the grid results in SSMS. It takes time
to populate the grid, and this affects the time difference between two queries. When
comparing two queries that each produce millions of rows, it is difficult to really see the
difference. Listing 4-8 shows an example of using STATISTICS TIME.

Listing 4-8. Use STATISTICS TIME To Compare Two Queries

```
--4-8.0 Settings
SET STATISTICS IO OFF;
SET STATISTICS TIME ON;
SET NOCOUNT ON;
GO

--4-8.1 The join query
PRINT '4-8.1';
SELECT SOH.CustomerID, SOH.SalesOrderID, SOH.OrderDate, C.TerritoryID,
    ROW_NUMBER() OVER(PARTITION BY SOH.CustomerID ORDER BY SOH.OrderDate)
        AS RowNumber
```

```
FROM Sales.SalesOrderHeader AS SOH
JOIN Sales.Customer C ON SOH.CustomerID = C.CustomerID;

--4-8.2 The CTE
PRINT '4-8.2';
WITH Sales AS (
    SELECT CustomerID, OrderDate, SalesOrderID,
        ROW_NUMBER() OVER(PARTITION BY CustomerID ORDER BY OrderDate)
            AS RowNumber
    FROM Sales.SalesOrderHeader)
SELECT Sales.CustomerID, SALES.SalesOrderID, Sales.OrderDate,
    C.TerritoryID, Sales.RowNumber
FROM Sales
JOIN Sales.Customer AS C ON C.CustomerID = Sales.CustomerID;
```

Figure 4-11 shows the messages tab scrolled down to the information specific to these queries. I ran the queries several times. Sometimes the first query ran faster; sometimes the second query ran faster. The results in the figure show Query 2 running slightly faster.

```
4-8.1

 SQL Server Execution Times:
   CPU time = 0 ms,   elapsed time = 0 ms.

 SQL Server Execution Times:
   CPU time = 93 ms,  elapsed time = 433 ms.
4-8.2

 SQL Server Execution Times:
   CPU time = 0 ms,   elapsed time = 0 ms.

 SQL Server Execution Times:
   CPU time = 63 ms,  elapsed time = 431 ms.
```

Figure 4-11. *The STATISTICS TIME for two queries*

You can also run a trace or use extended events to time queries. One solution I came up with for making time comparisons involves turning off the grid results and running the query many times within a loop. Turning off the grid results also turns off the messages, so you can't see STATISTICS IO or STATISTICS TIME. To find out how long each batch took, I look at the time at the bottom right of the SSMS output window.

To turn off the grid results, open the Options dialog from the Tools menu of SSMS. Expand Query Results. Expand SQL Server. Select Results to Grid. Check Discard results after execution and click OK. Figure 4-12 shows the Options dialog box.

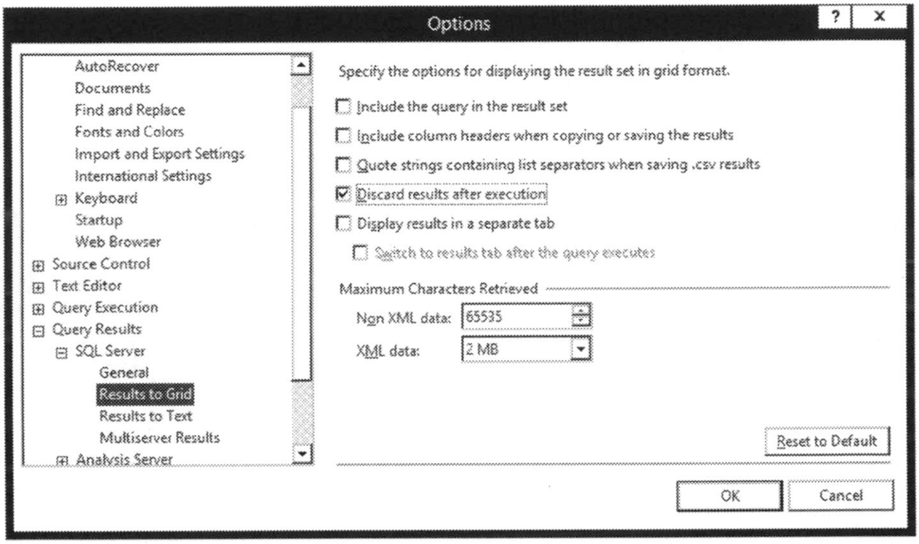

Figure 4-12. *Turning off grid results*

You will need to close SSMS and restart it for the setting to go into effect. Now run Listing 4-9 to see how long it takes to run a query with a join and a window function. Be sure to note the run time at the bottom of the window when the script is done.

Listing 4-9. Timing the First Query

```
--4-9.0 Set up a loop
DECLARE @count INT = 0;
WHILE @count < 1000 BEGIN
    --4-9.1 The query
    SELECT SOH.CustomerID, SalesOrderID, OrderDate, c.TerritoryID,
    ROW_NUMBER() OVER(PARTITION BY soh.CustomerID ORDER BY OrderDate)
        AS RowNumber
    FROM Sales.SalesOrderHeader AS SOH
    JOIN Sales.Customer C ON SOH.CustomerID = C.CustomerID;

    SET @count += 1;
END;
```

I ran the script multiple times. It took 39 to 45 seconds on my laptop to run Listing 4-9. Now run Listing 4-10. Again, note the time to run the script and make sure to delete Listing 4-9 or run the script in a second window.

Listing 4-10. Timing the Second Query

```
--4-10.0 Set up a loop
DECLARE @count INT = 0;
WHILE @count < 1000 BEGIN

    --4-10.1 The query
    WITH Sales AS (
        SELECT CustomerID, OrderDate, SalesOrderID,
            ROW_NUMBER() OVER(PARTITION BY CustomerID ORDER BY OrderDate)
                AS RowNumber
        FROM Sales.SalesOrderHeader)
    SELECT Sales.CustomerID, SALES.SalesOrderID, Sales.OrderDate, C.TerritoryID,
        Sales.RowNumber
    FROM Sales
    JOIN Sales.Customer AS C ON C.CustomerID = Sales.CustomerID;

    SET @count += 1;
END;
```

After running Listing 4-10 several times, it consistently ran at 26 seconds. For testing queries returning millions of rows, turning off the grid results is a useful technique. In this case, you may need to just run each query once to see the difference. To make sure that you are not comparing a warm cache to a cold one, clear the cache before running each query with DBCC DROPCLEANBUFFERS. Don't run this command on a production server, however!

If you wish to return the database back to its normal state, run Listing 4-11. Also, be sure to turn the grid results back on.

Listing 4-11. Cleaning Up the Database

```
--4-11.1 Drop index
DROP INDEX [IX_SalesOrderHeader_CustomerID_OrderDate]
    ON Sales.SalesOrderHeader;
GO

--4-11-2 Recreate original index
CREATE INDEX [IX_SalesOrderHeader_CustomerID] ON Sales.SalesOrderHeader
    (CustomerID);
```

Summary

You can affect the performance of queries with window functions by adding an index that sorts on the PARTITION BY and ORDER BY clauses. A properly constructed index can improve the performance of many queries containing window functions. You may have problems, however, with window aggregates due to the worktable created in tempdb. Be sure to test, though, before ruling out window aggregates. The difference between them and another technique is often negligible, and the window aggregate query is usually much easier to write. You may also have challenges with queries involving multiple tables.

In Chapter 5, you will begin learning about the window function enhancements added in 2012. I like to think that these features give SQL Server super powers!

CHAPTER 5

▓ ▓ ▓

Calculating Running and Moving Aggregates

Imagine you have been given the task of writing a T-SQL query with running totals of sales by customer. Maybe your first thought is to use a cursor to do it. Maybe you are familiar with some query techniques like self-joins to accomplish the task. If you are running SQL Server 2012 or later, you are in luck! Window functions make it easy to calculate running totals, moving averages, and more.

In this chapter, you will learn how adding an ORDER BY clause to a window aggregate changes everything! You will learn how to add calculations for running and moving aggregates, something often required in business reports and dashboards.

Adding ORDER BY to Window Aggregates

You learned how to use window aggregates to add summaries to queries without grouping in Chapter 3. The 2005 window aggregate functionality does not support the ORDER BY component in the OVER clause. Starting with SQL Server 2012, you can add an ORDER BY to a window aggregate to calculate running totals. To differentiate between this functionality and the 2005 functionality, this book will call the 2012 functionality *accumulating window aggregates*. When adding the ORDER BY, the window changes. Each row has a different window to operate on. The window is based on the ORDER BY expression. By default, the window consists of the first row in the results and includes all the subsequent rows up to the current row. Figure 5-1 demonstrates how the windows work.

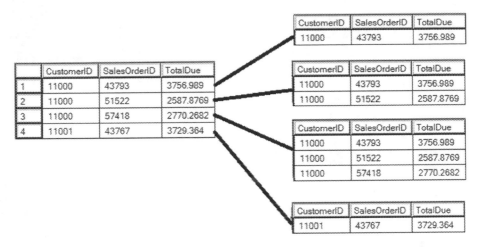

Figure 5-1. *Each row has a different window*

In the examples leading up to this chapter, the actual rows making up the windows were determined by the PARTITION BY expressions. In the case of accumulating aggregates, the PARTITION BY, ORDER BY, and a frame define which rows end up in the window. A frame can be used to more finely define the window. The example in this section uses the default frame. You will learn more about frames in the "Calculating Moving Totals and Averages" section in this chapter and even more in Chapter 6. Here is the syntax:

```
<AggregateFunction>(<col1>) OVER([PARTITION BY <expression>]
    ORDER BY <expression> [Frame definition])
```

Listing 5-1 demonstrates how to use accumulating window aggregates to calculate running totals.

Listing 5-1. Calculating Running Totals

```
--5-1.1 A running total
SELECT CustomerID, SalesOrderID, CAST(OrderDate AS DATE) AS OrderDate,
    TotalDue, SUM(TotalDue) OVER(PARTITION BY CustomerID
        ORDER BY SalesOrderID) AS RunningTotal
FROM Sales.SalesOrderHeader;
```

Figure 5-2 shows the partial results. The RunningTotal column values increase until reaching a different CustomerID. At that point, the totals start over.

	CustomerID	SalesOrderID	OrderDate	TotalDue	RunningTotal
1	11000	43793	2011-06-21	3756.989	3756.989
2	11000	51522	2013-06-20	2587.8760	6344.8659
3	11000	57418	2013-10-03	2770.2682	9115.1341
4	11001	43767	2011-06-17	3729.364	3729.364
5	11001	51493	2013-06-18	2674.0227	6403.3867
6	11001	72773	2014-05-12	650.8008	7054.1875
7	11002	43736	2011-06-09	3756.989	3756.989

Figure 5-2. Partial results of calculating running totals with accumulating aggregates

The OVER clause in the example shown in Listing 5-1 uses the default frame. By altering the frame, you can calculate moving aggregates.

Calculating Moving Totals and Averages

Moving totals and averages are very popular business and economic metrics. Developers may be asked to provide reports with these calculations over three months or over twelve months, for example. By default, the window for accumulating window aggregates keeps growing within the partition, but, for moving aggregates, you want the window size to stay the same. You can accomplish this by adding a frame definition. Here is the syntax for accumulating window aggregates including the frame for a moving aggregate. Chapter 6 covers framing extensively, so for now just copy the code in the examples.

```
<AggregateFunction>(<col1>) OVER([PARTITION BY <expression>]]
    ORDER BY <expression>
    [ROWS BETWEEN <number> PRECEDING AND CURRENT ROW])
```

The window is different for each row. Figure 5-3 demonstrates how the window works for a moving aggregate.

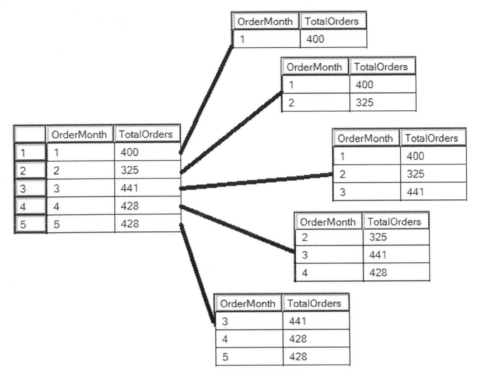

Figure 5-3. *The windows for a moving aggregate over three months*

Run Listing 5-2 to see an example.

Listing 5-2. Calculating Moving Averages and Sums

```
--5-2.1 Three month sum and average for products qty sold
SELECT MONTH(SOH.OrderDate) AS OrderMonth, SOD.ProductID, SUM(SOD.OrderQty)
AS QtySold,
    SUM(SUM(SOD.OrderQty))
    OVER(PARTITION BY SOD.ProductID ORDER BY MONTH(SOH.OrderDate)
    ROWS BETWEEN 2 PRECEDING AND CURRENT ROW) AS ThreeMonthSum,
    AVG(SUM(SOD.OrderQty))
    OVER(PARTITION BY SOD.ProductID ORDER BY MONTH(SOH.OrderDate)
    ROWS BETWEEN 2 PRECEDING AND CURRENT ROW) AS ThreeMonthAvg
FROM Sales.SalesOrderHeader AS SOH
JOIN Sales.SalesOrderDetail AS SOD ON SOH.SalesOrderID = SOD.SalesOrderID
JOIN Production.Product AS P ON SOD.ProductID = P.ProductID
WHERE OrderDate >= '2013-01-01' AND OrderDate < '2014-01-01'
GROUP BY MONTH(SOH.OrderDate), SOD.ProductID;
```

The query is filtered for orders placed in 2013 and aggregated to the month and ProductID. Figure 5-4 shows the partial results, one year's sales of product 707. Notice that the window function in each case is applied to an aggregate, the sum of OrderQty. When using a window function in an aggregate query, any columns used in the function or the OVER clause follow the same rules as the SELECT list. See the "Adding Window Aggregates to Aggregate Queries" section in Chapter 3 for more information. By adding ORDER BY and the ROWS expression (frame) to the OVER clause, the window moves forward and includes at most three rows each time.

	OrderMonth	ProductID	QtySold	ThreeMonthSum	ThreeMonthAvg
1	1	707	45	45	45
2	2	707	111	156	78
3	3	707	146	302	100
4	4	707	146	403	134
5	5	707	226	518	172
6	6	707	285	657	219
7	7	707	448	959	319
8	8	707	314	1047	349
9	9	707	320	1082	360
10	10	707	345	979	326
11	11	707	296	961	320
12	12	707	258	899	299

Figure 5-4. *Partial results of calculating moving aggregates*

Most of the time, the requirements for three month averages specify that the average should be NULL if there are not three months to average. For example, the averages for January and February would be NULL. Starting in March, the three months are available to average. You'll see how to address this in Chapter 9.

Solving Queries Using Accumulating Aggregates

Creating running and moving aggregates is very easy! You will learn how to take advantage of the frame component of the OVER clause in Chapter 6 to make sure that you get the very best performance. Unlike the ranking functions, calculating a running or moving aggregate may be the solution in itself, not just a step along the way to the solution. The following section shows how to use accumulating window functions to solve even more interesting problems.

The Last Good Value Problem

I ran across this problem in a forum, and several people tried to solve it. The best solution was developed by Itzik Ben-Gan.

The table for this problem has two columns. The first, ID, is an incrementing integer, the primary key of the table. The second column may contain NULL values. The task is to replace each NULL with the previous non-NULL value. Listing 5-3 creates and populates the table and displays the rows.

Listing 5-3. Creating and Populating the Table

```
--5-3.1 Create the table
CREATE TABLE #TheTable(ID INT, Data INT);

--5-3.2 Populate the table
INSERT INTO #TheTable(ID, Data)
VALUES(1,1),(2,1),(3,NULL),
    (4,NULL),(5,6),(6,NULL),
    (7,5),(8,10),(9,11);

--5-3.3 Display the results
SELECT * FROM #TheTable;
```

Figure 5-5 shows the raw data in the table. Notice that rows 3, 4, and 6 have NULL in the Data column. The solution will replace the NULL with 1 for rows 3 and 4, and with 6 for row 6.

	ID	Data
1	1	1
2	2	1
3	3	NULL
4	4	NULL
5	5	6
6	6	NULL
7	7	5
8	8	10
9	9	11

Figure 5-5. *The data for the last good value problem*

I found Itzik's solution to be quite elegant and brilliant. It takes advantage of the fact that you can use any of the aggregate functions as accumulating window aggregates, not just SUM and AVG. Take a look at row 4. The value needed to replace the NULL is the Data value from row 2. The ID of row 2 is also the maximum ID for the rows leading up to row 4 that are not NULL in the Data column. A window that starts at row 1 of a partition and goes up to the current row is the same window that you need for a running total! You can take advantage of this fact to find the maximum ID leading up to the current row where the Data value is not NULL. Listing 5-4 shows step 1 of this solution.

Listing 5-4. Step 1 of the Solution

```
5-4.1 Find the max non-null row
SELECT ID, Data,
    MAX(CASE WHEN Data IS NOT NULL THEN ID END)
    OVER(ORDER BY ID) AS MaxRow
FROM #TheTable;
```

Figure 5-6 shows the results so far. The MaxRow column is the ID from the row that contains the Data value that each row needs. The MAX function finds the largest ID value for rows that have a non-NULL Data value up to the current row.

	ID	Data	MaxRow
1	1	1	1
2	2	1	2
3	3	NULL	2
4	4	NULL	2
5	5	6	5
6	6	NULL	5
7	7	5	7
8	8	10	8
9	9	11	9

Figure 5-6. *The results of step 1*

My first thought is that I could use the MaxRow column to join the table to itself, but take a look at this data closely. Within each group of rows with the same MaxRow value, there is one non-NULL Data row, and the rest are NULL. There are three rows where MaxRow is 2. Only one of those rows has a non-NULL Data value. My next thought is to just group by MaxRow and use the MAX function on the Data column. The problem is that you would lose the details that you need to see by doing so. But, window aggregates let you add an aggregate function without changing the query to an aggregate query. Instead of grouping on MaxRow, partition on it. Listing 5-5 shows the complete solution.

Listing 5-5. The Complete Solution

```
--5-5.1 The solution
WITH MaxData AS
    (SELECT ID, Data,
        MAX(CASE WHEN Data IS NOT NULL THEN ID END)
        OVER(ORDER BY ID) AS MaxRow
    FROM #TheTable)
SELECT ID, Data,
    MAX(Data) OVER(PARTITION BY MaxRow) AS NewData
FROM MaxData;
```

Figure 5-7 shows the results. The first part of the solution is added to a CTE. In the outer query, the MAX function is used to find the maximum Data value, actually the only one that is not NULL, partitioned by the MaxRow.

	ID	Data	NewData
1	1	1	1
2	2	1	1
3	3	NULL	1
4	4	NULL	1
5	5	6	6
6	6	NULL	6
7	7	5	5
8	8	10	10
9	9	11	11

Figure 5-7. *The complete results of the Last Good Value Problem*

The solution seems quite simple once you see it. Thanks to Itzik Ben-Gan for figuring this out.

The Subscription Problem

The Subscription Problem was originally part of a contest in 2009 called the Speed Phreak Challenge from Simple-Talk.com. At that time, the latest version of SQL Server available was 2008. The object of the problem was to calculate the count of current subscriptions by month as subscribers joined and left over time. The requirements also stated to ignore future cancellations; in other words, ignore the months with cancellations but no new subscriptions. The data and a cursor-based solution were provided. The cursor-based solution running against 10,000 rows took 7 seconds on a typical laptop in 2009, while the winning solution took just a few milliseconds.

The power of both SQL Server and laptops has improved immensely since 2009. Six years later, the cursor-based solution took just 1 second to run on my laptop with 8GB of RAM and an SSD drive. The winning code took under 30 milliseconds. The winning solution was very difficult to understand, so Simple-Talk asked me to write an article explaining it shortly after the contest. Now that SQL Server 2012 and the accumulating window aggregate functions are available, will a new solution be easier to write and run faster? Here is your chance to find out.

The data, solutions, and explanations from 2009 can be found in the article at www.simple-talk.com/sql/performance/writing-efficient-sql-set-based-speed-phreakery/. You will need to follow the instructions found there to create and populate the data if you want to work though this example. To get started, take a look at the data by running Listing 5-6.

Listing 5-6. The Subscription Data

```
--5-6.1 The subscription data
SELECT *
FROM Registrations;
```

Figure 5-8 shows partial results with the grid scrolled down to see a cancellation.

	Registration_ID	FirstName	LastName	DateJoined	DateLeft
13	13	Allen	Hunter	2004-01-04 00:00:00.000	NULL
14	14	Marianne	West	2004-01-04 00:00:00.000	NULL
15	16	Gabriel	Serrano	2004-01-04 00:00:00.000	NULL
16	15	Norma	Lynch	2004-01-04 00:00:00.000	2008-08-20 00:00:00.000

Figure 5-8. *Partial view of the Registrations table*

Now armed with SQL Server 2012, the solution is very easy to write, and it performs even better than the original winning code. Listing 5-7 shows the new solution.

Listing 5-7. Solving the Subscription Problem with SQL Server 2012 Functionality

```
--5-7.1 Solve the subscription problem
WITH NewSubs AS (
    SELECT EOMONTH(DateJoined) AS TheMonth,
        COUNT(DateJoined) AS PeopleJoined
    FROM Registrations
    GROUP BY EOMONTH(DateJoined)),
 Cancelled AS (
    SELECT EOMONTH(DateLeft) AS TheMonth,
        COUNT(DateLeft) AS PeopleLeft
    FROM Registrations
    GROUP BY EOMONTH(DateLeft))
SELECT NewSubs.TheMonth AS TheMonth, NewSubs.PeopleJoined,
    Cancelled.PeopleLeft,
    SUM(NewSubs.PeopleJoined - ISNULL(Cancelled.PeopleLeft,0))
    OVER(ORDER BY NewSubs.TheMonth) AS Subscriptions
FROM NewSubs
LEFT JOIN Cancelled ON NewSubs.TheMonth = Cancelled.TheMonth;
```

The partial results, which match the answer from the contest, are shown in Figure 5-9. The first step is to get a count by month for new subscriptions and cancellations. To do that, the data must be grouped by month. In this case, the new EOMONTH function is used, which changes each date to the last day of the month. The original solutions on Simple-Talk returned the first day of the month. It is quite simple to change the dates to the first of each month if you want to do so. The important thing is that subscriptions and cancellations are grouped by month.

	TheMonth	PeopleJoined	PeopleLeft	Subscriptions
1	2004-01-31	167	NULL	167
2	2004-02-29	133	NULL	300
3	2004-03-31	144	NULL	444
4	2004-04-30	155	NULL	599
5	2004-05-31	156	NULL	755
6	2004-06-30	136	1	890
7	2004-07-31	138	NULL	1028
8	2004-08-31	132	NULL	1160
9	2004-09-30	163	NULL	1323
10	2004-10-31	135	NULL	1458

Figure 5-9. Partial results of the Subscription Problem

The new subscription and cancellation counts are separated into CTEs to get the PeopleJoined and PeopleLeft values, respectively, for each month. The outer query joins the NewSubs CTE to the Cancelled CTE with a LEFT JOIN because there are many months with no cancellations. The SUM of PeopleJoined minus PeopleLeft after PeopleLeft is corrected for NULL is calculated as a running total.

The query was very easy to write and runs pretty fast. It ran in 10 milliseconds on my laptop, even faster than the winning solution from 2009.

Summary

Starting with SQL Server 2012, adding an ORDER BY to the OVER clause changes a window aggregate into an accumulating window aggregate. This lets you easily create running totals plus moving totals and averages. You are not limited to using this functionality for just sums and averages, however. The MAX function was also used to solve a difficult problem.

You were briefly introduced to frames in this chapter when looking at moving sums and averages. Chapter 6 takes a deep look at frames.

CHAPTER 6

■ ■ ■

Adding Frames to the Window

You have looked through the window and used it to write some powerful queries. You have partitioned it like the smaller panes in a large window. Now you will learn how to create very granular windows, much like stained glass, with frames.

In this chapter, you will learn how framing, where it is supported, is so important to the performance of the queries and the accuracy of the results.

Understanding Framing

When the 2012 T-SQL features were first announced back in 2011, I must confess that framing intimidated me a bit. I didn't really like the syntax and didn't quite understand what was going on. Luckily, frames are only supported with specific window functions. The scariest things in life, like public speaking, often turn out to have the biggest payoffs, and framing in window function expressions is no different. Taking the time to understand framing will really help you get the best performance.

With framing, you can specify a window that is smaller than the partition. For example, you may want a window that starts at the first row of the set but stops at the current row. You may want a window that starts just 12 rows before the current row regardless of how many rows are in the partition. With frames, you can define windows that meet these special requirements.

Before you start adding frames to your OVER clauses, you should understand several key terms. Table 6-1 lists the terms and the definitions.

Table 6-1. *Key Framing Terms*

Key term	Definition
ROWS	A physical operator. Looks at the position of the rows.
RANGE	A logical operator, but not fully implemented in SQL Server 2012 and 2014. Looks at the value of an expression over the rows.
UNBOUNDED PRECEDING	The frame starts at the first row in the set.
UNBOUNDED FOLLOWING	The frame ends at the final row in the set.
N PRECEDING	A physical number of rows before the current row. Supported only with ROWS.
N FOLLOWING	A physical number of rows after the current row. Supported only with ROWS.
CURRENT ROW	The row of the current calculation.

You saw in Chapter 5 that the window for accumulating aggregates is different for every row. If you are calculating a running total, the window for row 1 is row 1. The window for row 2 is rows 1 and 2. The window for row 3 is rows 1 to 3, and so on. In each case, the window begins at the first row of the partition and ends at the current row. Figure 6-1 shows what the frames look like when partitioned by CustomerID. Notice that the window for row 4 is in a new partition, CustomerID 11001, and row 4 is the first row in that partition.

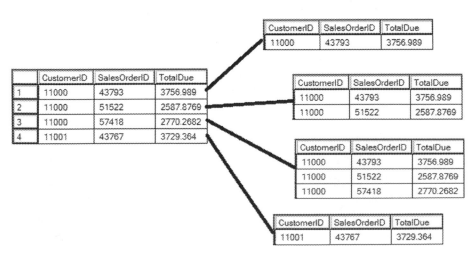

Figure 6-1. *Each row has a different window*

The frame definition consists of the keyword ROWS or RANGE followed by the word BETWEEN. Then you must specify a starting point and ending point. Here is the syntax:

```
ROWS BETWEEN <starting expression> AND <ending expression>
RANGE BETWEEN <starting expression> AND <ending expression>
```

There are two possible frame expressions that will give you an accumulating aggregate, like a running total, starting with the first row of the partition and ending with the current row: ROWS BETWEEN UNBOUNDED PRECEDING AND CURRENT ROW and RANGE BETWEEN UNBOUNDED PRECEDING AND CURRENT ROW. You will learn more about the differences between ROWS and RANGE later in the chapter, but for now, you should understand that RANGE BETWEEN UNBOUNDED PRECEDING AND CURRENT ROW is the default frame where a frame is supported and when one is not specified. That is why you can just add an ORDER BY expression to an OVER clause for SUM and produce a running total. The expressions SUM(TotalDue) OVER(ORDER BY OrderID) and SUM(TotalDue) OVER(ORDER BY OrderID RANGE BETWEEN UNBOUNDED PRECEDING AND CURRENT ROW) are equivalent.

For reasons that you will learn later in the chapter, the preferred frame expression uses ROWS instead of RANGE. You can also use an abbreviated syntax for the running total frame: ROWS UNBOUNDED PRECEDING.

To create a frame that starts at the current row and includes all of the rows to the end of the set, use ROWS BETWEEN CURRENT ROW AND UNBOUNDED FOLLOWING. This will allow you to create a reverse running total. Another way to use a frame is by specifying a number of rows to include in the frame. This syntax can only be used with ROWS. You can specify a number of rows before, after, or before and after the current row. There is also a shortcut for this expression if you intend a number of rows before the current row: ROWS <N> PRECEDING.

Imagine that you have a partition consisting of 10 rows, and that the current row is row 5. Table 6-2 lists several frame examples and the rows that the examples refer to.

Table 6-2. Framing Examples

Frame	Rows
ROWS BETWEEN 3 PRECEDING AND CURRENT ROW	2 - 5
ROWS BETWEEN CURRENT ROW AND 4 FOLLOWING	5 - 9
ROWS BETWEEN 3 PRECEDING AND 4 FOLLOWING	2 - 9
ROWS BETWEEN UNBOUNDED PRECEDING AND CURRENT ROW	1 - 5
ROWS BETWEEN CURRENT ROW AND UNBOUNDED FOLLOWING	5 - 10

Figure 6-2 illustrates these examples.

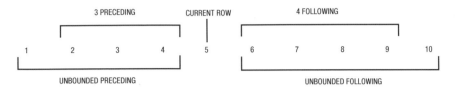

Figure 6-2. *Some framing examples*

Applying Frames to Running and Moving Aggregates

Frames were first introduced to SQL Server with the 2012 version. They apply to a subset of window functions, the accumulating aggregates you learned about in Chapter 5 and two of the offset functions, FIRST_VALUE and LAST_VALUE. You will learn about offset functions in Chapter 7.

By specifying the frame, you can calculate reverse running totals and moving aggregates. Run Listing 6-1 to see some examples.

Listing 6-1. Using Frames

```
--6-1.1 Running and reverse running totals
SELECT CustomerID, FORMAT(OrderDate,'yyyy-MM-dd') AS OrderDate,
SalesOrderID, TotalDue,
    SUM(TotalDue) OVER(PARTITION BY CustomerID ORDER BY SalesOrderID
    ROWS UNBOUNDED PRECEDING) AS RunningTotal,
    SUM(TotalDue) OVER(PARTITION BY CustomerID ORDER BY SalesOrderID
    ROWS BETWEEN CURRENT ROW AND UNBOUNDED FOLLOWING) AS ReverseTotal
FROM Sales.SalesOrderHeader
ORDER BY CustomerID, SalesOrderID;

--6.1-2 Moving sum and average
SELECT YEAR(OrderDate) AS OrderYear, MONTH(OrderDate) AS OrderMonth,
    COUNT(*) AS OrderCount,
    SUM(COUNT(*)) OVER(ORDER BY YEAR(OrderDate), MONTH(OrderDate)
    ROWS BETWEEN 2 PRECEDING AND CURRENT ROW) AS ThreeMonthCount,
    AVG(COUNT(*)) OVER(ORDER BY YEAR(OrderDate), MONTH(OrderDate)
    ROWS BETWEEN 2 PRECEDING AND CURRENT ROW) AS ThreeMonthAvg
FROM Sales.SalesOrderHeader
WHERE OrderDate >= '2012-01-01' AND OrderDate < '2013-01-01'
GROUP BY YEAR(OrderDate), MONTH(OrderDate);
```

Figure 6-3 shows the partial results. By specifying that the window should start at the current row and continue to the end of the partition, you can create a reverse running total as in Query 1. By specifying that the window is made up of two rows before the current row and the current row as in Query 2, you create a window that moves.

	CustomerID	OrderDate	SalesOrderID	TotalDue	RunningTotal	ReverseTotal
1	11000	2011-06-21	43793	3756.989	3756.989	9115.1341
2	11000	2013-06-20	51522	2587.8769	6344.8659	5358.1451
3	11000	2013-10-03	57418	2770.2682	9115.1341	2770.2682
4	11001	2011-06-17	43767	3729.364	3729.364	7054.1875
5	11001	2013-06-18	51493	2674.0227	6403.3867	3324.8235
6	11001	2014-05-12	72773	650.8008	7054.1875	650.8008

	OrderYear	OrderMonth	OrderCount	ThreeMonthCount	ThreeMonthAvg
1	2012	1	336	336	336
2	2012	2	219	555	277
3	2012	3	304	859	286
4	2012	4	269	792	264
5	2012	5	293	866	288
6	2012	6	390	952	317

Figure 6-3. *Partial results of using frames*

Measuring Performance

If you look at the execution plan when running a query with an accumulating window aggregate, you will see a *Window Spool* operator. The Window Spool operator creates a work table for performing the calculations. In some cases, the work table will be created in tempdb, but sometimes it will be created in memory. When it is created in memory, there are no locks and no I/O. It is extremely efficient. Unfortunately, you can't tell where the work table lives when you look at the execution plan. The only way you can really tell what is going on is by looking at STATISTICS IO in addition to the plan. Turn on the graphical execution plan by typing CTRL + M and run Listing 6-2 to see the difference between the two types of frames.

Listing 6-2. Comparing Frame Types

```
--6-2.0 Settings
SET STATISTICS IO ON;
SET NOCOUNT ON;
GO
```

```
--6-2.1 Using the default RANGE
PRINT '6-2.1'
SELECT CustomerID, SalesOrderID,
    SUM(TotalDue) OVER(PARTITION BY CustomerID ORDER BY SalesOrderID)
        AS RunningTotal
FROM Sales.SalesOrderHeader;

--6-2.2 Using ROWS
PRINT '6-2.1'
SELECT CustomerID, SalesOrderID,
    SUM(TotalDue) OVER(PARTITION BY CustomerID ORDER BY SalesOrderID
    ROWS UNBOUNDED PRECEDING) AS RunningTotal
FROM Sales.SalesOrderHeader;
```

Query 1 does not specify the frame. By default, it uses RANGE to define the frame. Query 2 uses the ROWS option. If you look at the execution plans, partially shown in Figure 6-4, you will see that they are similar, but not identical. Each has a Window Spool operator. The Window Spool operator for Query 1 is misleading because the work table is actually created in tempdb.

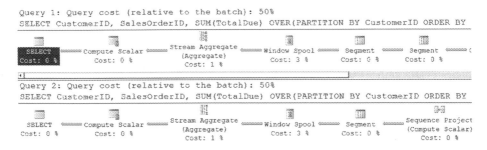

Figure 6-4. *Partial execution plans comparing ROWS and RANGE*

The execution plans report that the relative cost for each query is 50%. Take a look at the logical reads reported in the Messages tab and shown in Figure 6-5. Each query read 689 pages, which is the total number of pages in the table. Query 1 took 188,791 logical reads from a work table, while Query 2 took 0 logical reads. Why the difference? The work table in Query 1 was created in tempdb, and the work table in Query 2 was created in memory.

```
6-2.1
Table 'Worktable'. Scan count 50584, logical reads 188791, phy
Table 'SalesOrderHeader'. Scan count 1, logical reads 689, phy
6-2.2
Table 'Worktable'. Scan count 0, logical reads 0, physical rea
Table 'SalesOrderHeader'. Scan count 1, logical reads 689, phy
```

Figure 6-5. *The STATISTICS IO from the queries comparing ROWS and RANGE*

When looking at the I/O information, it is obvious that ROWS performs much better than RANGE. One really important thing to keep in mind is that, if you do not specify the frame, RANGE will be used. If you turn off STATISTICS IO and replace it with STATISTICS TIME instead, you can also see that Query 1 takes twice as long to run as Query 2. Figure 6-6 shows the STATISTICS TIME information.

```
6-2.1

 SQL Server Execution Times:
   CPU time = 0 ms,  elapsed time = 0 ms.

 SQL Server Execution Times:
   CPU time = 594 ms,  elapsed time = 766 ms.
6-2.2

 SQL Server Execution Times:
   CPU time = 0 ms,  elapsed time = 0 ms.

 SQL Server Execution Times:
   CPU time = 172 ms,  elapsed time = 383 ms.
```

Figure 6-6. *The STATISTICS TIME information comparing ROWS and RANGE*

When presenting window functions at SQL Server events throughout the US, I preach to the audience to forget RANGE, and always use ROWS. Until RANGE is fully implemented according to the standards, there is really no reason to use it. There is also a logical difference, which you will learn about in the next section. You may be wondering how the performance of accumulating window aggregates compares to older techniques even when using the default, RANGE. Run Listing 6-3 to find out.

Listing 6-3. Comparing the Default Frame to Older Techniques

```
--6-3.0 Set up
SET STATISTICS IO ON;
SET NOCOUNT ON;
GO

--6-3.1 Using the default frame
PRINT '6-3.1'
SELECT CustomerID, SalesOrderID,
    SUM(TotalDue) OVER(PARTITION BY CustomerID
    ORDER BY SalesOrderID) AS RunningTotal
FROM Sales.SalesOrderHeader;
```

```
--6-3.2 Correlated subquery
PRINT '6-3.2'
SELECT CustomerID, SalesOrderID,
    (SELECT SUM(TotalDue)
    FROM Sales.SalesOrderHeader AS IQ
    WHERE IQ.CustomerID = OQ.CustomerID
        AND IQ.SalesOrderID >= OQ.SalesOrderID)
    AS RunningTotal
FROM Sales.SalesOrderHeader AS OQ;

--6-3.3 CROSS APPLY
PRINT '6-3.3'
SELECT OQ.CustomerID, OQ.SalesOrderID, CA.RunningTotal
FROM Sales.SalesOrderHeader AS OQ
CROSS APPLY (
    SELECT SUM(TotalDue) AS RunningTotal
    FROM Sales.SalesOrderHeader AS IQ
    WHERE IQ.CustomerID = OQ.CustomerID
        AND IQ.SalesOrderID >= OQ.SalesOrderID) AS CA;
```

If you take a look at the Messages tab, you can see that using the default frame in Query 1 to calculate running totals uses more I/O than the older techniques used in Query 2 and Query 3. The performance of the older techniques is not great, either. The lesson here is to always specify the frame where it is supported and use ROWS.

In some situations, you may find that the work table ends up in tempdb even when you use ROWS. This could be due to a very large number of rows in the partitions or possibly by using expressions other than column names in the OVER clause.

You have seen how the frame affects the performance. What happens when more than one window aggregate is added to the query? When the OVER clauses are identical, the windows are reused and there is no performance penalty. Run Listing 6-4 to see how this works.

Listing 6-4. Queries with Multiple Window Functions

```
--6-4.0 Set up
SET STATISTICS IO ON;
SET NOCOUNT ON;
GO

--6-4.1
PRINT '6-4.1'
SELECT CustomerID, SalesOrderID,
    SUM(TotalDue) OVER(PARTITION BY CustomerID ORDER BY SalesOrderID
    RANGE UNBOUNDED PRECEDING) AS RunningSum
FROM Sales.SalesOrderHeader;
```

```
--6-4.2 Two window functions, same OVER
PRINT '6-4.1'
SELECT CustomerID, SalesOrderID,
    SUM(TotalDue) OVER(PARTITION BY CustomerID ORDER BY SalesOrderID
    RANGE UNBOUNDED PRECEDING) AS RunningSum,
    AVG(TotalDue) OVER(PARTITION BY CustomerID ORDER BY SalesOrderID
    RANGE UNBOUNDED PRECEDING) AS RunningAvg
FROM Sales.SalesOrderHeader;

--6-4.3 Two window functions, different OVER
PRINT '6-4.3'
SELECT CustomerID, SalesOrderID,
    SUM(TotalDue) OVER(PARTITION BY CustomerID ORDER BY SalesOrderID
    RANGE UNBOUNDED PRECEDING) AS RunningSum,
    AVG(TotalDue) OVER(ORDER BY SalesOrderID
    RANGE UNBOUNDED PRECEDING) AS RunningAvg
FROM Sales.SalesOrderHeader;
```

Query 1 has one accumulating window aggregate expression using a RANGE frame in the OVER clause. Query 2 has two accumulating window aggregate expression using the same OVER clause in each. Query 3 has two accumulating window aggregate expressions with different OVER clauses. If you review the STATISTICS IO on the Messages tab, you see that the I/O for Queries 1 and 2 are identical. Query 3 took twice as much I/O because it couldn't reuse the window.

Understanding the Logical Difference Between ROWS and RANGE

You have seen that ROWS has a big performance advantage over RANGE and you may be wondering why. You must understand the logical difference between the two operators first. The ROWS operator is a physical operator, while the RANGE operator is a logical one. This is very similar to the difference between ROW_NUMBER and RANK. When there are ties in the ORDER BY expression, RANK will repeat the value while ROW_NUMBER will give a unique value. If there are ties in the ORDER BY expression of the OVER clause when calculating running totals, ROWS and RANGE will return different results as well. Run Listing 6-5 to see this difference.

Listing 6-5. The Difference Between ROWS and RANGE

```
--6-5.1 Compare the logical difference between ROWS and RANGE
SELECT CustomerID, CAST(OrderDate AS DATE) AS OrderDate, SalesOrderID,
TotalDue,
    SUM(TotalDue) OVER(ORDER BY OrderDate
        ROWS UNBOUNDED PRECEDING) AS RunningTotalRows,
    SUM(TotalDue) OVER(ORDER BY OrderDate
        RANGE UNBOUNDED PRECEDING) AS RunningTotalRange
FROM Sales.SalesOrderHeader
WHERE CustomerID =11300
ORDER BY SalesOrderID;
```

The partial results are shown in Figure 6-7. The ORDER BY expressions in the OVER clauses are both OrderDate, which is not unique. Take a look at rows 7 and 8 where the customer has placed two orders on the same day. The RunningTotalRows values increment as expected while the RunningTotalRange value is the same for both rows. On row 9, the RunningTotalRange value lines back up again.

	CustomerID	OrderDate	SalesOrderID	TotalDue	RunningTotalRows	RunningTotalRange
1	11300	2013-07-03	52035	45.957	45.957	45.957
2	11300	2013-07-04	52083	35.6694	81.6264	81.6264
3	11300	2013-08-04	53835	101.1959	182.8223	182.8223
4	11300	2013-08-14	54388	82.8529	265.6752	265.6752
5	11300	2013-08-19	54662	8.7848	274.46	274.46
6	11300	2013-09-20	56487	38.664	313.124	313.124
7	11300	2013-10-21	58365	97.7483	410.8723	453.8347
8	11300	2013-10-21	58370	42.9624	453.8347	453.8347
9	11300	2013-11-14	60130	9.934	463.7687	463.7687
10	11300	2013-12-06	61611	66.8194	530.5881	530.5881

Figure 6-7. *Partial results of comparing ROWS to RANGE*

The window for ROWS in this case starts with the first row and includes all rows up to the current row sorted by the ORDER BY. The window for RANGE is all rows starting with the first row and up to any rows with the *same value* as the current row's ORDER BY expression. When the window for row 7 is determined, RANGE looks at not just the position but also the value. The value for the OrderDate for row 8 is the same as the value for row 7, so row 8 is included in the window for row 7. The optimizer can't tell how many rows will be in the window for RANGE ahead of time and creates the work tables in tempdb.

Just in case you think there is a bug with RANGE, run Listing 6-6, which uses one of the older techniques and returns the identical results to using RANGE.

Listing 6-6. Same Results from Older Technique

```
--6-6.1 Look at the older technique
SELECT CustomerID, CAST(OrderDate AS DATE) AS OrderDate,
    SalesOrderID, TotalDue,
    (SELECT SUM(TotalDue)
    FROM Sales.SalesOrderHeader AS IQ
    WHERE IQ.CustomerID = OQ.CustomerID
        AND IQ.OrderDate <= OQ.OrderDate) AS RunningTotal
FROM Sales.SalesOrderHeader AS OQ
WHERE CustomerID =11300
ORDER BY SalesOrderID;
```

The partial results are shown in Figure 6-8. Take a look at rows 7 and 8. You'll see that because the OrderDate values are the same, the RunningTotal values are the same as well.

	CustomerID	OrderDate	SalesOrderID	TotalDue	RunningTotal
1	11300	2013-07-03	52035	45.957	45.957
2	11300	2013-07-04	52083	35.6694	81.6264
3	11300	2013-08-04	53835	101.1959	182.8223
4	11300	2013-08-14	54388	82.8529	265.6752
5	11300	2013-08-19	54662	8.7848	274.46
6	11300	2013-09-20	56487	38.664	313.124
7	11300	2013-10-21	58365	97.7483	453.8347
8	11300	2013-10-21	58370	42.9624	453.8347
9	11300	2013-11-14	60130	9.934	463.7687
10	11300	2013-12-06	61611	66.8194	530.5881

Figure 6-8. *Partial results of using an older technique to calculate running totals*

The RANGE operator is really meant to work with logical sets such as months or quarters. This functionality has been defined by the standard but is not implemented at this time. In the meantime, make sure you always specify the frame with ROWS.

Summary

It's easy to write a query that calculates running totals or moving averages. If you don't understand framing, however, you will not get the best performance. By default, the frame is defined with RANGE, but ROWS almost always performs better.

Luckily, you do not have to worry about the frame except when using accumulating window aggregates and the functions FIRST_VALUE and LAST_VALUE. You will learn about FIRST_VALUE and LAST_VALUE in the next chapter, Chapter 7.

CHAPTER 7

■ ■ ■

Taking a Peek at Another Row

Along with accumulating window aggregates, Microsoft added eight new window functions with SQL Server 2012. Four of the functions, which I'll call offset functions in this book, are my favorite T-SQL functions, and they are LAG, LEAD, FIRST_VALUE, and LAST_VALUE. These functions let you include any columns from other rows in your results without a self-join and with fantastic performance.

In this chapter, you will learn how to use LAG, LEAD, FIRST_VALUE, and LAST_VALUE. You will see how easy they are to use and how great they perform.

Understanding LAG and LEAD

You saw how to use LAG in Chapter 1 to solve the stock market problem. Based on the ORDER BY expression of the OVER clause, you can use LAG to include a column from a row earlier in the results and LEAD to include a column later in the results. Framing is not supported with LAG and LEAD, so you don't have to worry about performance most of the time. Partitioning is optional, just as for other window functions, and ORDER BY is required. Here is the basic syntax:

```
LAG (<column you need>) OVER([PARTITION BY <expression>] ORDER BY <expression>)
LEAD (<column you need>) OVER([PARTITION BY <expression>] ORDER BY <expression>)
```

Run Listing 7-1 to see LAG and LEAD in action.

Listing 7-1. Using LAG and LEAD

```
--7-1.1 Use LAG and LEAD
SELECT CustomerID, SalesOrderID, CAST(OrderDate AS DATE) AS OrderDate,
    LAG(CAST(OrderDate AS DATE)) OVER(PARTITION BY CustomerID
        ORDER BY SalesOrderID) AS PrevOrderDate,
    LEAD(CAST(OrderDate AS DATE)) OVER(PARTITION BY CustomerID
        ORDER BY SalesOrderID) AS NextOrderDate
FROM Sales.SalesOrderHeader;
```

```
--7-1.2 Use LAG and LEAD as an argument
SELECT CustomerID, SalesOrderID, CAST(OrderDate AS DATE) AS OrderDate,
    DATEDIFF(DAY,LAG(OrderDate)
        OVER(PARTITION BY CustomerID ORDER BY SalesOrderID), OrderDate)
        AS DaysSincePrevOrder,
    DATEDIFF(DAY, OrderDate, LEAD(OrderDate)
        OVER(PARTITION BY CustomerID ORDER BY SalesOrderID))
        AS DaysUntilNextOrder
FROM Sales.SalesOrderHeader;
```

Figure 7-1 shows the partial results. Query 1 uses the LAG and LEAD functions to find the previous and next order dates relative to the current row. The argument for the functions is the OrderDate cast to the DATE data type. Just like the other window functions, PARTITION BY is optional. In this case, the data is partitioned by the CustomerID. The ORDER BY is a very important part of the OVER clause. It determines which row is the previous row and which row is the next row. Query 2 has the same OVER clauses as Query 1. The difference is that the LAG and LEAD expressions are used as arguments to the DATEDIFF functions to determine the number of days between orders.

	CustomerID	SalesOrderID	OrderDate	PrevOrderDate	NextOrderDate
1	11000	43793	2011-06-21	NULL	2013-06-20
2	11000	51522	2013-06-20	2011-06-21	2013-10-03
3	11000	57418	2013-10-03	2013-06-20	NULL
4	11001	43767	2011-06-17	NULL	2013-06-18
5	11001	51493	2013-06-18	2011-06-17	2014-05-12
6	11001	72773	2014-05-12	2013-06-18	NULL

	CustomerID	SalesOrderID	OrderDate	DaysSincePrevOrder	DaysUntilNextOrd...
1	11000	43793	2011-06-21	NULL	730
2	11000	51522	2013-06-20	730	105
3	11000	57418	2013-10-03	105	NULL
4	11001	43767	2011-06-17	NULL	732
5	11001	51493	2013-06-18	732	328
6	11001	72773	2014-05-12	328	NULL

Figure 7-1. *Partial results of the LAG and LEAD functions*

Note that there are several NULL values in the results. Row 1 is the first row of the partition. You cannot find an earlier row, so NULL is returned for PrevOrderDate and DaysSincePrevOrder. Row 3 is the final row of the partition. There is no row past Row 3 in the partition so NextOrderDate and DaysUntilNextOrder are null for Row 3.

So far, you have seen the default ways to use LAG and LEAD. These functions each have two optional parameters. The first parameter is the Offset, which is 1 by default. By default, LEAD pulls an expression from one row before the current row, and LAG pulls an expression from one row past the current row. By using the Offset parameter, you can access columns from rows farther away than one. One interesting thing to note about the offset is that only positive integers are allowed. When using LAG, a positive number means "go backward." When using LEAD, a positive number means "go forward." Here is the syntax for using the Offset parameter:

```
LAG(<column>  [,<offset>]) OVER(<over clause expression>)
LEAD(<column> [,<offset>]) OVER(<over clause expression>)
```

Listing 7-2 demonstrates how to use the Offset parameter.

Listing 7-2. Using the Offset Parameter with LAG

```
--7-2.1 Using Offset with LAG
WITH Totals AS (
    SELECT YEAR(OrderDate) AS OrderYear,
        MONTH(OrderDate)/4 + 1 AS OrderQtr,
        SUM(TotalDue) AS TotalSales
        FROM Sales.SalesOrderHeader
    GROUP BY YEAR(OrderDate), MONTH(OrderDate)/4 + 1)
SELECT OrderYear, Totals.OrderQtr, TotalSales,
    LAG(TotalSales, 4) OVER(ORDER BY OrderYear, OrderQtr)
        AS PreviousYearsSales
FROM Totals
ORDER BY OrderYear, OrderQtr;
```

Figure 7-2 shows the results. In this example, the total is aggregated by the year and calendar quarter in a CTE. The calendar quarter is calculated by finding the month, dividing by four and adding one. In the outer query, by using LAG with an offset of four, the previous year's sales for the same quarter are returned. Note that this method will only work if there are no gaps in the data, since it is using a physical offset and not a logical one. To prove that the results are correct, compare the PreviousYearSales of row 8, the first quarter of 2013, to the TotalSales of row 4, the first quarter of 2102.

	OrderYear	OrderQtr	TotalSales	PreviousYearsSales
1	2011	2	3366300.3016	NULL
2	2011	3	9326950.3248	NULL
3	2011	4	1462448.8986	NULL
4	2012	1	9443736.8161	NULL
5	2012	2	13775726.6319	3366300.3016
6	2012	3	11279388.6953	9326950.3248
7	2012	4	3176848.1687	1462448.8986
8	2013	1	8771886.3577	9443736.8161
9	2013	2	17746902.2275	13775726.6319
10	2013	3	17886522.2822	11279388.6953
11	2013	4	4560577.0958	3176848.1687
12	2014	1	14373277.4766	8771886.3577
13	2014	2	8046220.8391	17746902.2275

Figure 7-2. *The results of using the Offset with LAG*

The first four rows of the results return NULL for the PreviousYearSales. That is because there is no row with an offset of four from the current row until you get to row 5. If returning NULLs is a problem, you can use the second optional parameter to replace NULLs with a default value. In order to use the second parameter, you must also fill in the first parameter. Here is the syntax:

```
LAG(<column> [,<offset>] [,<default>]) OVER(<over clause expression>)
LEAD(<column> [,<offset>] [,<default>]) OVER(<over clause expression>)
```

Listing 7-3 demonstrates how to use the Default parameter.

Listing 7-3. Using the Default Parameter with LAG

```
--7-3.1 Using Offset with LAG
WITH Totals AS (
    SELECT YEAR(OrderDate) AS OrderYear,
        MONTH(OrderDate)/4 + 1 AS OrderQtr,
        SUM(TotalDue) AS TotalSales
        FROM Sales.SalesOrderHeader
    GROUP BY YEAR(OrderDate), MONTH(OrderDate)/4 + 1)
SELECT OrderYear, Totals.OrderQtr, TotalSales,
    LAG(TotalSales, 4, 0) OVER(ORDER BY OrderYear, OrderQtr)
        AS PreviousYearsSales
FROM Totals
ORDER BY OrderYear, OrderQtr;
```

Figure 7-3 shows the results. This query is the same as the query from Listing 7-2 with the addition of the Default parameter. All NULL values in PreviousYearSales have been changed to zero. Of course, you can use both the Offset and Default with LEAD as well.

	OrderYear	OrderQtr	TotalSales	PreviousYearsSales
1	2011	2	3366300.3016	0.00
2	2011	3	9326950.3248	0.00
3	2011	4	1462448.8986	0.00
4	2012	1	9443736.8161	0.00
5	2012	2	13775726.6319	3366300.3016
6	2012	3	11279388.6953	9326950.3248
7	2012	4	3176848.1687	1462448.8986
8	2013	1	8771886.3577	9443736.8161
9	2013	2	17746902.2275	13775726.6319
10	2013	3	17886522.2822	11279388.6953
11	2013	4	4560577.0958	3176848.1687
12	2014	1	14373277.4766	8771886.3577
13	2014	2	8046220.8391	17746902.2275

Figure 7-3. *The results using the Default parameter with LAG*

Understanding FIRST_VALUE and LAST_VALUE

While LAG and LEAD allow you to include any column from a row a given number of rows away from the current row, the FIRST_VALUE and LAST_VALUE functions let you include any column from the first or last row of the partition. At first glance, this may seem very similar to MIN and MAX, but they are very different. The column to sort on is not necessarily the column to pull into the results. The first value may not be the minimum value. These functions do not have any optional parameters, but they do support framing. Review Chapter 6 to learn more about framing if you are not familiar with the concept. Recall that the default frame starts at the first row of the partition and includes all rows up to the current row. This causes a problem when using LAST_VALUE. If you do not specify the frame, LAST_VALUE returns the value from the current row instead of from the last row of the partition. That is because the current row is the same as the last row with the default frame. Listing 7-4 demonstrates how to use FIRST_VALUE and LAST_VALUE.

Listing 7-4. Using FIRST_VALUE and LAST_VALUE

```
--7-4.1 Using FIRST_VALUE and LAST_VALUE
SELECT CustomerID, SalesOrderID, TotalDue,
    FIRST_VALUE(TotalDue) OVER(PARTITION BY CustomerID
        ORDER BY SalesOrderID) AS FirstOrderAmt,
    LAST_VALUE(TotalDue) OVER(PARTITION BY CustomerID
        ORDER BY SalesOrderID) AS LastOrderAmt_WRONG,
    LAST_VALUE(TotalDue) OVER(PARTITION BY CustomerID
        ORDER BY SalesOrderID
        ROWS BETWEEN CURRENT ROW AND UNBOUNDED FOLLOWING) AS LastOrderAmt
FROM Sales.SalesOrderHeader
ORDER BY CustomerID, SalesOrderID;
```

Figure 7-4 shows the partial results. The windows are partitioned by CustomerID and ordered by SalesOrderID. The query itself is ordered by CustomerID and SalesOrderID so you can verify the results. Take a look at row 2. The FirstOrderAmt correctly returns the value of the TotalDue from row 1. The window frame for FirstOrderAmt is the default, all rows from the beginning of the partition up to the current row. Since the frame was not specified for LastOrderAmt_WRONG, the frame is the same, which only goes up to the current row. The query was intending to pull a value from the very last row of the partition, however. In order to do that, the frame must be specified. The expression for LastOrderAmt includes the correct frame so it actually does return the expected value.

	CustomerID	SalesOrderID	TotalDue	FirstOrderAmt	LastOrderAmt_WRONG	LastOrderAmt
1	11000	43793	3756.989	3756.989	3756.989	2770.2682
2	11000	51522	2587.8769	3756.989	2587.8769	2770.2682
3	11000	57418	2770.2682	3756.989	2770.2682	2770.2682
4	11001	43767	3729.364	3729.364	3729.364	650.8008
5	11001	51493	2674.0227	3729.364	2674.0227	650.8008
6	11001	72773	650.8008	3729.364	650.8008	650.8008
7	11002	43736	3756.989	3756.989	3756.989	2673.0613
8	11002	51238	2535.964	3756.989	2535.964	2673.0613

Figure 7-4. *Partial results of using FIRST_VALUE and LAST_VALUE*

Using the Offset Functions to Solve Queries

My favorite T-SQL functions of all time are LAG and LEAD. Not only are they easy to use, but they perform very well, too. You will learn more about how the performance of the offset functions compares to other methods in the next section. Now you will see how offset functions can be used to solve some real-world problems.

The Year-Over-Year Growth Calculation

Year-over-year (YOY) growth is a very commonly used metric in business. It compares a period, such as a month or quarter, to the same period from the previous year. Run Listing 7-5 to see how easy this is to do with LAG.

Listing 7-5. Calculating YOY Growth with LAG

```
--7-5.1 Calculate Year-Over-Year Growth
WITH
Level1 AS (
    SELECT YEAR(OrderDate) AS SalesYear,
        MONTH(OrderDate) AS SalesMonth,
        SUM(TotalDue) AS TotalSales
    FROM Sales.SalesOrderHeader
    GROUP BY YEAR(OrderDate), MONTH(OrderDate)
    ),
Level2 AS (
    SELECT SalesYear, SalesMonth,TotalSales,
        LAG(TotalSales,12) OVER(ORDER BY SalesYear) AS PrevYearSales
    FROM Level1)
SELECT SalesYear, SalesMonth,FORMAT(TotalSales,'C') AS TotalSales,
    FORMAT(PrevYearSales,'C') AS PrevYearSales,
    FORMAT((TotalSales-PrevYearSales)/PrevYearSales,'P') AS YOY_Growth
FROM Level2
WHERE PrevYearSales IS NOT NULL;
```

Figure 7-5 shows the partial results. In order to demonstrate a stepwise approach, this query contains two CTEs. Except for filtering out the NULL values, the same results could be obtained by writing the query at two levels, but I think this approach makes it easier to understand. The first CTE, Level1, creates a list of sales by year and month. Level2 adds in the expression using LAG to calculate the sales for the same month of the previous year. Finally, in the outer query, the YOY calculation is performed by subtracting the previous year's sales from the current sales and dividing by the previous year's sales. The FORMAT function is used to change the results to a percentage. The rows that cannot be compared to a previous row are filtered out of the outer query.

	SalesYear	SalesMonth	TotalSales	PrevYearSales	YOY_Growth
1	2012	3	$3,336,347.47	$1,462,448.90	128.13 %
2	2012	9	$3,881,724.19	$507,096.47	665.48 %
3	2012	8	$2,442,451.18	$554,791.61	340.24 %
4	2012	2	$1,649,051.90	$5,156,269.53	-68.01 %
5	2012	11	$2,097,153.13	$2,292,182.88	-8.50 %
6	2012	7	$3,840,231.46	$567,020.95	577.26 %
7	2012	5	$3,452,924.45	$2,800,576.17	23.29 %
8	2012	10	$2,858,060.20	$815,313.02	250.54 %

Figure 7-5. *Partial results of calculating YOY growth*

The Gaps Problem

In Chapter 2, you saw how to solve the Islands problem by using a ranking function. You can build on that solution using LAG to solve the "gaps" part of the problem. Data that should be contiguous, but is missing some values, can be queried to find islands (sections of contiguous rows) and gaps (sections of missing values). To understand how to solve the Islands problem, review the "Solving the Islands Problem" section in Chapter 2. Run Listing 7-6 to create a temp table and display the islands in the data.

Listing 7-6. Populating the Data and Viewing the Islands

```
--7-6.1 Create the #Islands table
CREATE TABLE #Islands(ID INT NOT NULL ) ;

--7-6.2 Populate the #Islands table
INSERT INTO #Islands(ID)
VALUES(1),(2),(3),(6),(8),(8),(9),(10),(11),(12),(12),(14),(15),(18),(19);

--7-6.3 The Islands
WITH Islands AS (
    SELECT ID, DENSE_RANK() OVER(ORDER BY ID) AS DenseRank,
        ID - DENSE_RANK() OVER(ORDER BY ID) AS Diff
    FROM #Islands)
SELECT MIN(ID) AS IslandStart, MAX(ID) AS IslandEnd
FROM Islands
GROUP BY Diff;
```

Figure 7-6 shows the results.

	IslandStart	IslandEnd
1	1	3
2	6	6
3	8	12
4	14	15
5	18	19

Figure 7-6. *The Islands*

Each gap starts after an island ends and ends before a new island starts. For example, the first gap is 4 to 5. That is one more than the end of the first island, 3, and one less than the beginning of the second island, 6. By applying LEAD to the islands solution, you can calculate the gaps. Listing 7-7 shows how this can be done. Be sure to run Listing 7-7 in the same query window as Listing 7-6 so that the temp table is still available.

Listing 7-7. Returning the Gaps

```
--7-7.1 Find the Gaps
WITH
Level1 AS (
    SELECT ID, DENSE_RANK() OVER(ORDER BY ID) AS DenseRank,
        ID - DENSE_RANK() OVER(ORDER BY ID) AS Diff
    FROM #Islands),
Level2 AS (
    SELECT MIN(ID) AS IslandStart, MAX(ID) AS IslandEnd
    FROM Level1
    GROUP BY Diff),
Level3 AS (
    SELECT IslandEnd + 1 AS GapStart,
        LEAD(IslandStart) OVER(ORDER BY IslandStart) -1 AS GapEnd
    FROM Level2)
SELECT GapStart, GapEnd
FROM Level3
WHERE GapEnd IS NOT NULL;
```

Figure 7-7 shows the results. The outer query of the islands solution is moved to a CTE, Level2. Inside CTE Level3, one is added to the IslandEnd to calculate the beginning of each gap. To calculate the end of each gap, the LEAD function is used to retrieve the IslandStart value from the next row. By subtracting one, the end of the gap can be found. In the outer query, the GapEnd column is filtered to remove an unneeded row that will show up after the last island.

	GapStart	GapEnd
1	4	5
2	7	7
3	13	13
4	16	17

Figure 7-7. *The Gaps*

Comparing Performance

You have seen how offset functions can provide easy and elegant solutions. Of course, you usually have to pay a performance penalty for simplicity. Luckily, that is not the case with the offset functions. There are a couple of exceptions that will be explained in this section, but most of the time they offer amazing performance.

LAG and LEAD Performance

It is difficult to write queries that accomplish the same thing as LAG and LEAD. To find the row next to the current row, you can use TOP(1) along with a correlated subquery or OUTER APPLY. Toggle on the execution plan (CTRL + M) and run Listing 7-8 to see how LAG compares to traditional queries.

Listing 7-8. Comparing the Performance of LAG

```
--7-8.0 Set up
SET STATISTICS IO ON;
SET NOCOUNT ON;
GO

--7-8.1 Use LAG and LEAD
PRINT '7-8.1'
SELECT CustomerID, SalesOrderID, CAST(OrderDate AS DATE) AS OrderDate,
    LAG(CAST(OrderDate AS DATE)) OVER(PARTITION BY CustomerID
        ORDER BY SalesOrderID)
        AS PrevOrderDate
FROM Sales.SalesOrderHeader;

--7-8.2 Use Correlated Subquery
PRINT '7-8.2'
SELECT CustomerID, SalesOrderID, CAST(OrderDate AS DATE) AS OrderDate,
    (SELECT TOP(1) CAST(OrderDate AS DATE)
    FROM Sales.SalesOrderHeader AS IQ
```

```
    WHERE IQ.CustomerID = OQ.CustomerID
        AND IQ.SalesOrderID < OQ.SalesOrderID
    ORDER BY SalesOrderID) AS PrevOrderDate
FROM Sales.SalesOrderHeader AS OQ;

--7-8.3 Use OUTER APPLY
PRINT '7-8.3'
SELECT CustomerID, SalesOrderID, CAST(OrderDate AS DATE) AS OrderDate,
    OA.PrevOrderDate
FROM Sales.SalesOrderHeader AS OQ
OUTER APPLY (
    SELECT TOP(1) CAST(OrderDate AS DATE) AS PrevOrderDate
    FROM Sales.SalesOrderHeader AS IQ
    WHERE IQ.CustomerID = OQ.CustomerID
        AND IQ.SalesOrderID < OQ.SalesOrderID
    ORDER BY SalesOrderID) AS OA;
```

If you take a look at the Messages tab shown in Figure 7-8, you will see that the LAG method takes just a few hundred logical reads compared to over 100,000 for each of the other techniques. The execution plan also reports that Query 1 took only 10% of the resources needed for the batch.

```
7-8.1
Table 'Worktable'. Scan count 0, logical reads 0, physical reads 0
Table 'SalesOrderHeader'. Scan count 1, logical reads 689, physica
7-8.2
Table 'SalesOrderHeader'. Scan count 31474, logical reads 100784,
Table 'Worktable'. Scan count 0, logical reads 0, physical reads 0
7-8.3
Table 'SalesOrderHeader'. Scan count 31474, logical reads 100784,
Table 'Worktable'. Scan count 0, logical reads 0, physical reads 0
```

Figure 7-8. *The logical reads compared to LAG*

Most of the time, LAG and LEAD perform very well. You can improve the performance by adding an index on the PARTTION BY and ORDER BY columns. Review Chapter 4 to learn more about this index, which eliminates sorting and decreases the logical reads. There is one exception to the great performance, however. It is possible to use an expression instead of a hard-coded value for the optional Offset parameter. In this case, the engine will create a worktable in tempdb instead of in memory because it doesn't know the size of the window ahead of time. The execution plan will still show a Window Spool operator, so you will need to look at the logical reads to know what is going on. Listing 7-9 demonstrates this issue.

Listing 7-9. LAG with an Expression in the Offset Argument

```
--7-9.0 Set up
SET STATISTICS IO ON;
SET NOCOUNT ON;
GO

--7-9.1 A dynamic offset
DECLARE @Offset INT = 1;
SELECT CustomerID, SalesOrderID, CAST(OrderDate AS DATE) AS OrderDate,
    LAG(CAST(OrderDate AS DATE),@Offset) OVER(PARTITION BY CustomerID
        ORDER BY SalesOrderID) AS PrevOrderDate
FROM Sales.SalesOrderHeader;
```

Figure 7-9 shows the Messages tab. In this case, even though it is obvious that the offset equals 1 for all rows, the worktable is created in tempdb. Instead of just 689 logical reads, or 119 if you have the special index in place, there are 188,791 logical reads for the worktable.

```
Table 'Worktable'. Scan count 50584, logical reads 188791,
Table 'SalesOrderHeader'. Scan count 1, logical reads 689,
```

Figure 7-9. *The logical reads for LAG when the offset is dynamic*

FIRST_VALUE and LAST_VALUE PERFORMANCE

Just like LAG and LEAD, FIRST_VALUE and LAST_VALUE can provide fantastic performance. The FIRST_VALUE and LAST_VALUE functions do not have an offset argument, but they do support framing. You saw in the "Understanding FIRST_VALUE and LAST_VALUE" section in this chapter that you must supply the frame for LAST_VALUE to get the expected results. Even though you get the expected results without specifying the frame with FIRST_VALUE, you should type out the frame to get better performance. Be sure to review Chapter 6 to learn more about framing. Listing 7-10 demonstrates the performance difference.

Listing 7-10. Comparing FIRST_VALUE Performance

```
--7-10.0 Set up
SET STATISTICS IO ON;
SET NOCOUNT ON;
GO
```

```
--7-10.1 Default frame
PRINT '7-10.1'
SELECT CustomerID, SalesOrderID, TotalDue,
    FIRST_VALUE(TotalDue) OVER(PARTITION BY CustomerID
    ORDER BY SalesOrderID) AS FirstOrderAmt
FROM Sales.SalesOrderHeader
ORDER BY CustomerID, SalesOrderID;

--7-10.2 ROWS
PRINT '7-10.2'
SELECT CustomerID, SalesOrderID, TotalDue,
    FIRST_VALUE(TotalDue) OVER(PARTITION BY CustomerID
    ORDER BY SalesOrderID ROWS UNBOUNDED PRECEDING) AS FirstOrderAmt
FROM Sales.SalesOrderHeader
ORDER BY CustomerID, SalesOrderID;
```

Figure 7-10 shows the Messages tab and logical reads. Query 1 uses the default frame, RANGE BETWEEN UNBOUNDED PRECEDING AND CURRENT ROW. The logical reads value is very high. By switching to ROWS instead, as in Query 2, the logical reads for the worktable are just zero. You can also add an index to improve the performance. Review Chapter 4 for more information about the index.

```
7-10.1
Table 'Worktable'. Scan count 50584, logical reads 188791,
Table 'SalesOrderHeader'. Scan count 1, logical reads 689,
7-10.2
Table 'Worktable'. Scan count 0, logical reads 0, physical
Table 'SalesOrderHeader'. Scan count 1, logical reads 689,
```

Figure 7-10. *The logical reads when the frame is specified*

Summary

The offset functions of LAG, LEAD, FIRST_VALUE, and LAST_VALUE available with SQL Server 2012 are very powerful. They not only make it easy to write queries that pull values from different rows, but the performance is fantastic, too!

There is one more set of functions to learn, the statistical functions. Chapter 8 teaches you what you need to know to take advantage of these window functions.

CHAPTER 8

■ ■ ■

Understanding Statistical Functions

In 2012, Microsoft added four more window functions to SQL Server. These are statistical functions PERCENT_RANK, CUME_DIST, PERCENTILE_CONT, and PERCENTILE_DISC. These functions make analyzing data from many sources, such as science, academics, or sports, easy.

In this chapter you will learn how to use these statistical functions.

Using PERCENT_RANK and CUME_DIST

Remember those standardized tests you took in school? You were probably given a raw score and a percent for each area tested, such as mathematics or language skills. Percent rank is a way to calculate how each individual in a group compares to the rest of the group.

Starting with SQL Server 2012, there are two functions for ranking data such as those test scores, or even heights. Say that there are 100 third graders lined up by height. My grandson, Thomas, is a pretty tall boy so he would stand at spot 95. He is taller than 94 other students. His height is higher than 94% of the heights, and is higher than or the same as 95% of the heights. Thomas' height has a PERCENT_RANK of 0.9494 and a CUME_DIST (cumulative distribution) of 0.95.

You may be wondering why the PERCENT_RANK is 0.9494 and not just 0.94. The formula for PERCENT_RANK is the rank of the score minus one divided by the number of scores minus one: (rank-1)/(N-1). The formula for CUME_DIST is just the rank of the score divided by the number of scores: rank/N. The PERCENT_RANK of Thomas' height can be found by dividing 94 by 99, not 94 by 100.

Just like all other window functions, an OVER clause is required when using these functions. It must contain an ORDER BY expression that determines how the scores or values are lined up. The PARTITION BY expression is optional. If it is used, then the items within a partition will be compared, not outside the partition. Here is the syntax:

```
PERCENT_RANK OVER([PARTITION BY <expression>] ORDER BY <expression>)
CUME_DIST OVER([PARTITION BY <expression>] ORDER BY <expression>)
```

Listing 8-1 demonstrates how to use these functions to compare the sales for each month of a given year.

Listing 8-1. Using PERCENT_RANK and CUME_DIST

```
--8-1.1 Using PERCENT_RANK and CUME_DIST
SELECT COUNT(*) NumberOfOrders, Month(OrderDate) AS OrderMonth,
    RANK() OVER(ORDER BY COUNT(*)) AS Ranking,
    PERCENT_RANK() OVER(ORDER BY COUNT(*)) AS PercentRank,
    CUME_DIST() OVER(ORDER BY COUNT(*)) AS CumeDist
FROM Sales.SalesOrderHeader
WHERE OrderDate >= '2013-01-01' AND OrderDate < '2014-01-01'
GROUP BY  Month(OrderDate);
```

Figure 8-1 shows the results. The query is filtered to include the orders for just 2013 and grouped by month. The ORDER BY expression for each function is the count of the orders. Recall that when you use a window function in an aggregate query, any columns used in the function must follow the rules for the SELECT list. See Chapter 3 for more information about adding a window function to an aggregate query. The PercentRank for the first row is zero. The first value for PercentRank will always be zero because that row is not ranked above any other row. Both the PercentRank and CumeDist will be 1, or 100% for the last row. In all rows except for the last, the CumeDist is larger than the PercentRank. Notice that when there is a tie, as in rows 3 and 4, the values are repeated.

	NumberOfOrders	OrderMonth	Ranking	PercentRank	CumeDist
1	325	2	1	0	0.0833333333333333
2	400	1	2	0.0909090909090909	0.166666666666667
3	428	4	3	0.181818181818182	0.333333333333333
4	428	5	3	0.181818181818182	0.333333333333333
5	441	3	5	0.363636363636364	0.416666666666667
6	719	6	6	0.454545454545455	0.5
7	1740	7	7	0.545454545454545	0.583333333333333
8	1789	8	8	0.636363636363636	0.666666666666667
9	1791	9	9	0.727272727272727	0.75
10	1968	10	10	0.818181818181818	0.833333333333333
11	2050	12	11	0.909090909090909	0.916666666666667
12	2103	11	12	1	1

Figure 8-1. *The results of using PERCENT_RANK and CUME_DIST*

Using PERCENTILE_CONT and PERCENTILE_DISC

You have seen how to rank and compare a series of values with PERCENT_RANK and CUME_DIST. The other two statistical functions, PERCENTILE_CONT (percentile continuous) and PERCENTILE_DISC (percentile discrete), perform the opposite task. Given a percent rank, these functions find the value at that position. The difference between these two functions is that PERCENTILE_CONT interpolates a value over the set while PERCENTILE_DISC returns a value from the set.

One very common requirement is to find the median, or middle value in a list of values. You can accomplish this task by using one of these functions and specifying that you wish to find the value at 50%.

The syntax of these functions is also a bit different compared to the other window functions. You still need to supply an OVER clause, but inside the OVER clause you only specify the PARTITION BY expression if one is needed. There is a new clause called WITHIN GROUP, where the ORDER BY will go, and the ORDER BY expression must evaluate to a numeric type like INT or DECIMAL. Here is the syntax:

```
PERCENTILE_CONT(<percent to find>) WITHIN GROUP(ORDER BY <expression>)
    OVER([PARTITION BY <expression>])
PERCENTILE_DISC(<percent to find>) WITHIN GROUP(ORDER BY <expression>)
    OVER([PARTITION BY <expression>])
```

For the results shown in Figure 8-1, what is the median? Since an even number of rows is returned, it is the average of 719 and 1740, or 1229.5. Listing 8-2 demonstrates how the median can be calculated with PERCENTILE_CONT and PERCENTILE_DISC.

Listing 8-2. Finding the Median with PERCENTILE_CONT and PERCENTILE_DISC

```
--8-2.1 Find median for the set
SELECT COUNT(*) NumberOfOrders, Month(OrderDate) AS orderMonth,
    PERCENTILE_CONT(.5) WITHIN GROUP (ORDER BY COUNT(*))
    OVER() AS PercentileCont,
    PERCENTILE_DISC(.5) WITHIN GROUP (ORDER BY COUNT(*))
    OVER() AS PercentileDisc
FROM Sales.SalesOrderHeader
WHERE OrderDate >= '2013-01-01' AND OrderDate < '2014-01-01'
GROUP BY Month(OrderDate);

--8-2.2 Return just the answer
SELECT  DISTINCT PERCENTILE_CONT(.5) WITHIN GROUP (ORDER BY COUNT(*))
    OVER() AS PercentileCont,
    PERCENTILE_DISC(.5) WITHIN GROUP (ORDER BY COUNT(*))
    OVER() AS PercentileDisc
FROM Sales.SalesOrderHeader
WHERE OrderDate >= '2013-01-01' AND OrderDate < '2014-01-01'
GROUP BY Month(OrderDate);
```

The results are shown in Figure 8-2. Query 1 shows the count and month for the entire year along with the `PercentileCont` and `PercentileDisc`. The values are the same for every row because the answer, the median, is the same for every row in the set. Query 2 removes the count and month and uses `DISTINCT` so that just the answers are returned. Notice that the `PercentileCont` interpolates the answer by averaging the two middle values. The `PercentileDisc`, however, returns a value of 719. This is an actual value in the set. If the number of values is even, then this function will return the first value closest to the median.

	NumberOfOrders	orderMonth	PercentileCont	PercentileDisc
1	325	2	1229.5	719
2	400	1	1229.5	719
3	428	4	1229.5	719
4	428	5	1229.5	719
5	441	3	1229.5	719
6	719	6	1229.5	719
7	1740	7	1229.5	719
8	1789	8	1229.5	719
9	1791	9	1229.5	719
10	1968	10	1229.5	719
11	2050	12	1229.5	719

	PercentileCont	PercentileDisc
1	1229.5	719

Figure 8-2. Finding the median

When there is an odd number of rows, these functions will return the same value when calculating the median. Listing 8-3 shows what happens if there is an odd number of rows by filtering out one month.

Listing 8-3. Finding the Median with an Odd Number of Rows

```
--8-3.1 Filter out January
SELECT  DISTINCT PERCENTILE_CONT(.5) WITHIN GROUP (ORDER BY COUNT(*))
    OVER() AS PercentileCont,
    PERCENTILE_DISC(.5) WITHIN GROUP (ORDER BY COUNT(*))
    OVER() AS PercentileDisc
FROM Sales.SalesOrderHeader
WHERE OrderDate >= '2013-02-01' AND OrderDate < '2014-01-01'
GROUP BY Month(OrderDate);
```

Figure 8-3 shows the results. In this case, since the number of rows is odd, the two functions return the same value.

	PercentileCont	PercentileDisc
1	1740	1740

Figure 8-3. *The two functions return the same median with odd rows*

While finding the median is probably the most common use for these functions, you can also use them to find the value at any other percent rank. A useful application of this would be to return the value at the top 25% position, for example. Listing 8-4 creates and populates a temp table with student scores and returns the score found at the top 25% position.

Listing 8-4. Finding the Score at the Top 25% Position

```
--8-4.1 Set up variables and table
DECLARE @score DECIMAL(5,2)
DECLARE @count INT = 1;
CREATE TABLE #scores(StudentID INT IDENTITY, Score DECIMAL(5,2));

--8-4.2 Loop to generate 1000 scores
WHILE @count <= 1000 BEGIN
    SET @score = CAST(RAND() * 100 AS DECIMAL(5,2));
    INSERT INTO #scores(Score )
    VALUES  (@score);

    SET @count +=1;
END;

--8-4.3 Return the score at the top 25%
SELECT DISTINCT PERCENTILE_DISC(.25) WITHIN GROUP
    (ORDER BY Score DESC) OVER() AS Top25
FROM #scores;
```

Figure 8-4 shows the result. Your value will be different, of course, since the scores were generated randomly. After setting up the variables and the table, a loop generates 1,000 insert statements with a random value. Query 3 returns the score at the top 25% position by finding the score with PERCENTILE_DISC 0.25 and sorting the scores in descending order.

	Top25
1	74.97

Figure 8-4. *The score at the top 25% position*

Comparing Statistical Functions to Older Methods

The functions PERCENT_RANK and CUME_DIST are more of a convenience than an amazing breakthrough like the offset functions you learned about in Chapter 7. By using the RANK function in a simple calculation, you can come up with the same answers. The formulas are as follows:

```
PERCENT_RANK = (Rank - 1)/(N - 1)
CUME_DIST = Rank/N
```

Listing 8-5 demonstrates that you can get the same results as Listing 8-1 by using SQL Server 2005 functionality.

Listing 8-5. Using SQL Server 2005 Functionality for the Same Results

```
--8-5.1 Using 2005 functionality
SELECT COUNT(*) NumberOfOrders, Month(OrderDate) AS OrderMonth,
    ((RANK() OVER(ORDER BY COUNT(*)) -1) * 1.0)/(COUNT(*) OVER() -1)
    AS PercentRank,
    (RANK() OVER(ORDER BY COUNT(*)) * 1.0)/COUNT(*) OVER()
    AS CumeDist
FROM Sales.SalesOrderHeader
WHERE OrderDate >= '2013-01-01' AND OrderDate < '2014-01-01'
GROUP BY  Month(OrderDate);
```

Figure 8-5 shows the results. Except that the zeros are filled out to 12 places, the results look the same. In this example, the window aggregate, COUNT(*) OVER, is used to calculate the number of rows in the partition. For PercentRank, one is subtracted from both the rank and the count before dividing.

	NumberOfOrders	OrderMonth	PercentRank	CumeDist
1	325	2	0.000000000000	0.083333333333
2	400	1	0.090909090909	0.166666666666
3	428	4	0.181818181818	0.250000000000
4	428	5	0.181818181818	0.250000000000
5	441	3	0.363636363636	0.416666666666
6	719	6	0.454545454545	0.500000000000
7	1740	7	0.545454545454	0.583333333333
8	1789	8	0.636363636363	0.666666666666
9	1791	9	0.727272727272	0.750000000000
10	1968	10	0.818181818181	0.833333333333
11	2050	12	0.909090909090	0.916666666666
12	2103	11	1.000000000000	1.000000000000

Figure 8-5. The results of calculating percents with older methods

You may be wondering about the performance, especially since the older method used a window aggregate that is not known for robust performance. When comparing the two methods, in this situation with no partitioning, the older method actually performed a bit better. Figure 8-6 shows the logical reads from the two queries.

```
Using 2005 functionality
Table 'Worktable'. Scan count 3, logical reads 29, physica
Table 'Workfile'. Scan count 0, logical reads 0, physical
Table 'SalesOrderHeader'. Scan count 1, logical reads 689,
Using PERCENT_RANK and CUME_DIST
Table 'Worktable'. Scan count 15, logical reads 100, physic
Table 'Workfile'. Scan count 0, logical reads 0, physical
Table 'SalesOrderHeader'. Scan count 1, logical reads 689,
```

Figure 8-6. The logical reads from the two methods

Is it possible to use an older method for the PERCENTILE_CONT and PERCENTILE_DISC functions? It is not difficult for PERCENTILE_DISC because it always returns an actual value from the set. Listing 8-6 shows how to calculate PERCENTILE_DISC using only 2005 functionality.

103

Listing 8-6. Using Only SQL Server 2005 Functionality to Calculate PERCENTILE_DISC

```
--8-6.1 PERCENTILE_DISC
SELECT DISTINCT PERCENTILE_DISC(0.75) WITHIN GROUP (ORDER BY COUNT(*))
OVER() AS PercentileDisc
FROM Sales.SalesOrderHeader
WHERE OrderDate >= '2013-01-01' AND OrderDate < '2014-01-01'
GROUP BY Month(OrderDate);

--8-6.2 Old method
WITH Level1 AS (
    SELECT COUNT(*) NumberOfOrders,
        ((RANK() OVER(ORDER BY COUNT(*)) -1) * 1.0)/(COUNT(*) OVER() -1)
        AS PercentRank
    FROM Sales.SalesOrderHeader
    WHERE OrderDate >= '2013-01-01' AND OrderDate < '2014-01-01'
    GROUP BY Month(OrderDate))
SELECT TOP(1) NumberOfOrders AS PercentileDisc
FROM Level1
WHERE Level1.PercentRank <= 0.75
ORDER BY Level1.PercentRank DESC;
```

Figure 8-7 shows the results. Query 1 uses the new functionality so that you can compare it to the older method. Query 2 moves the query to calculate the percent rank to a CTE called Level1. In the outer query, one row that is equal to or less than the percent rank 0.75 is returned.

	PercentileDisc
1	1791

	PercentileDisc
1	1791

Figure 8-7. *The result of using an older method for PERCENTILE_DISC*

Accomplishing the same thing for PERCENTILE_CONT is trickier, but can still be done. In this case, when the exact row is not available, a value is calculated by using one value above and one value below the given percent rank. When trying to find the median, you just average the two rows, but not when trying to find any other percent rank. The best formula I have found was to multiply the percent rank times the difference between the two values and then subtract from the larger value. Listing 8-7 shows the solution.

Listing 8-7. Finding PERCENTILE_CONT Using SQL Server 2005 Functionality

```
--8-7.1 PERCENTILE_CONT
SELECT DISTINCT PERCENTILE_CONT(0.75) WITHIN GROUP (ORDER BY COUNT(*))
OVER() AS PercentCont
FROM Sales.SalesOrderHeader
WHERE OrderDate >= '2013-01-01' AND OrderDate < '2014-01-01'
GROUP BY  Month(OrderDate);


--8-7.2 Using 2005 functionality
WITH
Level1 AS (
    SELECT COUNT(*) NumberOfOrders,
        CAST((RANK() OVER(ORDER BY COUNT(*)) -1)AS FLOAT)/
            (COUNT(*) OVER() -1)
        AS PercentRank
    FROM Sales.SalesOrderHeader
    WHERE OrderDate >= '2013-01-01' AND OrderDate < '2014-01-01'
    GROUP BY  Month(OrderDate)),
Level2 AS (
    SELECT numberoforders, SIGN(percentrank- 0.75) AS SGN,
        ROW_NUMBER() OVER(PARTITION BY SIGN(PercentRank - 0.75)
        ORDER BY ABS(PercentRank - 0.75))  AS rownumber
    FROM Level1),
Level3 AS(
    SELECT SUM(CASE WHEN SGN = 0 THEN NumberOfOrders END) AS ExactRow,
        SUM(CASE WHEN SGN = -1 THEN NumberOfOrders END) AS LowerRow,
        SUM(CASE WHEN SGN = 1 THEN NumberOfOrders END) AS UpperRow
    FROM level2
    WHERE rownumber = 1)
SELECT CASE WHEN ExactRow IS NOT NULL THEN ExactRow
    ELSE UpperRow - (UpperRow - LowerRow) * 0.75 END AS PercentCont
FROM Level3;
```

Figure 8-8 shows the results. Query 1 uses the PERCENTILE_CONT function so that you can compare to the older method. Query 2 moves the query to find PercentRank to a CTE called Level1. The query in Level2 uses the SIGN function to see if the value in each row is greater than, less than, or equal to 0.75. It returns 1, –1, or 0. This value is also used to partition a row number. The rows needed for the results will all have a row number of 1. The query in Level3 uses CASE to pivot the values into one row. The outer query uses a CASE expression to check for the exact value. If the exact value doesn't exist, then the formula using the two close rows is used.

	PercentCont
1	1835.25

	PercentCont
1	1835.25

Figure 8-8. *Comparing PERCENTILE_CONT to an older method*

The performance of the two queries was very close. Obviously, the new method is much, much easier to understand and write.

Summary

Now that you have seen statistical functions PERCENT_RANK, CUME_DIST, PERCENTILE_DISC, and PERCENTILE_CONT, you have used all of the window functions available with SQL Server 2012 and 2014. In Chapter 9, you will take a look at more real-world applications of window functions.

CHAPTER 9

■ ■ ■

Time Range Calculations and Trends

A common reporting requirement is to produce totals by different ranges of time for comparison. Typical reports contain totals by month, quarter, and year, sometimes with comparisons to the same period in the prior year or for month-to-date or year-to-date totals. Products like SQL Server Analysis Services and PowerPivot provide functions to navigate date hierarchies. With window functions in SQL Server 2012 or later, you can produce the same calculations using the techniques provided earlier in this book.

In this chapter, you will put all the techniques you have learned previously to work to create calculations for the following:

- Percent of Parent

- Year-to-Date (YTD)

- Quarter-to-Date (QTD)

- Month-to-Date (MTD)

- Same Period Prior Year (SP PY)

- Prior Year-to-Date (PY YTD)

- Moving Total (MT)

- Moving Average (MA)

Putting It All Together

You learned about using window aggregates to add summaries to queries without grouping in Chapter 3, accumulating aggregates in Chapter 5, and frames in Chapter 6. You will be putting these all together, with a bit of common sense, to create complex calculations that without the use of window functions would have required many more steps.

Remember, in the case of accumulating aggregates, PARTITION BY and ORDER BY determine which rows end up in the window. The FRAME DEFINITION is used to define the subset of rows from within the partition that will be aggregated. The examples in this section use the frame definition to do the heavy lifting. To review, here's the syntax:

```
<AggregateFunction>(<col1>) OVER([PARTITION BY <col2>[,<col3>,...<colN>]]
    ORDER BY <col4>[,<col5>,...<colN>] [Frame definition])
```

In this chapter, you will need to use the AdventureWorksDW sample database.

Percent of Parent

Comparing the performance of a product in a specific period to the performance for all products in that same period is a common analytic technique. In this next set of examples, you will build upon a simple base query by adding columns that calculate the pieces needed to produce the final Percent of Parent results. You will start out with a straightforward query that aggregates sales by month, and will add new calculation columns as they are covered, enabling each new column to be introduced on its own without needing to replicate the entire block of example code for each iteration. The code for the base query is shown in Listing 9-1 and the results are shown in Figure 9-1.

Listing 9-1. Base Query

```
SELECT f.ProductKey,
    YEAR(f.orderdate) AS OrderYear,
    MONTH(f.orderdate) AS OrderMonth,
    SUM(f.SalesAmount) AS [Sales Amt]
FROM dbo.FactInternetSales AS f
WHERE OrderDate BETWEEN '2011-01-01' AND '2012-12-31'
GROUP BY f.ProductKey,
    YEAR(f.orderdate),
    MONTH(f.orderdate)
ORDER BY 2, 3, f.ProductKey;
```

	ProductK...	OrderY...	OrderMo...	Sales Amt
1	310	2011	1	78721.94
2	311	2011	1	78721.94
3	312	2011	1	96613.29
4	313	2011	1	53674.05
5	314	2011	1	60830.59
6	322	2011	1	699.0982

Figure 9-1. *Results of the simple base query*

Ratio-to-Parent calculations can be generally defined as [Child Total] / [Parent Total]. In order to calculate the ratio as defined, you need to calculate the numerator and denominator inputs, and combine them in a third measure. To calculate the overall contribution each product has made to all sales, you need to determine the total for [All Sales] and for [Product All Sales]. Once you have those defined, you can calculate [Product % of All Sales] as [Product All Sales] / [All Sales]. You can multiply the resulting ratio by 100 to display it as a percentage, or rely on the formatting functions in the reporting or front-end tool to display them as percentages.

For each of these measures, the window aggregate SUM() function encapsulates a regular SUM() function, which might look a little bit strange to begin with, but is required to aggregate [SalesAmount] to levels higher than the level of granularity of the query. The result is the ability to aggregate the same source column to different levels in a single query without having to resort to temporary tables or common table expressions.

Listing 9-2 contains the additional column logic you need to append to the base query, just after the last column in the select list. Be sure to include a comma after [Sales Amt]. See Figure 9-2 for the results.

Listing 9-2. Additional Column Logic

```
SUM(SUM(f.SalesAmount)) OVER () AS [All Sales],
SUM(SUM(f.SalesAmount)) OVER (PARTITION BY f.productkey)
    AS [Product All Sales],
SUM(SUM(f.SalesAmount)) OVER (PARTITION BY f.productkey)
    / SUM(SUM(f.SalesAmount)) OVER()
    AS [Product % of All Sales]
```

	ProductKey	OrderYear	OrderMonth	Sales Amt	All Sales	Product All Sales	Product % of All Sales
1	310	2011	1	78721.94	12918011.1243	1195142.18	0.0925
2	311	2011	1	78721.94	12918011.1243	1001915.60	0.0775
3	312	2011	1	96613.29	12918011.1243	1198720.45	0.0927
4	313	2011	1	53674.05	12918011.1243	1077059.27	0.0833
5	314	2011	1	60830.59	12918011.1243	1052011.38	0.0814
6	322	2011	1	699.0982	12918011.1243	11884.6694	0.0009
7	324	2011	1	699.0982	12918011.1243	11185.5712	0.0008
8	326	2011	1	1398.1964	12918011.1243	15380.1604	0.0011
9	328	2011	1	699.0982	12918011.1243	18176.5532	0.0014

Figure 9-2. *Results of calculating product sales as a percentage of all sales*

The frame for the [All Sales] column does not have a PARTITION clause, which means it will aggregate across all the data available to the query, providing a total of sales for all time. This value will be the same for each row in the resulting table. The PARTITION clause for the [Product All Sales] column restricts the partition to each instance of a product key, providing a total of sales by product for all time. This value will be the same for all rows sharing the same [ProductKey] value.

The [Product % of All Sales] column combines the two prior statements to calculate the ratio between them. The key thing to realize is that you can combine the results of multiple aggregation results within a single column. Knowing this will allow you to create all manner of complex calculations that otherwise would have been relegated to a reporting tool or application code.

This approach works best if you work out the logic for each input component for a given calculation, then create the complex calculation that leverages the input calculations. The column calculations for the Annual and Monthly levels follow a similar pattern, so once you have calculations for one level worked out, the rest will follow quickly.

There is no need to worry about handling a divide-by-zero error at the "all" level, as the only case that will result in an error is if there are no rows at all in the source table, but for every level below it, you must account for situations where the denominator value can be zero. The calculations for the "annual" and "month" levels demonstrate how this can be done. By wrapping the window SUM() statement in a NULLIF() function, any zero aggregate values are turned into a NULL value, avoiding the divide-by-zero error. You could also use a CASE statement instead of NULLIF(). See Listing 9-3.

Listing 9-3. Additional Columns to Calculate the Annual and Monthly Percentage of Parent Columns

```
SUM(SUM(f.SalesAmount))
    OVER (PARTITION BY YEAR(f.OrderDate)) AS [Annual Sales],
SUM(SUM(f.SalesAmount))
    OVER (PARTITION BY f.productkey, YEAR(f.OrderDate))
    AS [Product Annual Sales],
--Pct of group:
--[Product % Annual Sales] = [Product Annual Sales] / [Annual Sales]
SUM(SUM(f.SalesAmount))
    OVER (PARTITION BY f.productkey, YEAR(f.OrderDate))
    / NULLIF(SUM(SUM(f.SalesAmount))
            OVER (PARTITION BY YEAR(f.OrderDate))
        , 0) AS [Product % Annual Sales],
SUM(SUM(f.SalesAmount))
    OVER (PARTITION BY YEAR(f.OrderDate), MONTH(f.OrderDate))
    AS [Month All Sales],
SUM(SUM(f.SalesAmount))
    OVER (PARTITION BY f.productkey, YEAR(f.OrderDate),
            MONTH(f.OrderDate))
    / NULLIF(SUM(SUM(f.SalesAmount))
            OVER (PARTITION BY YEAR(f.OrderDate), MONTH(f.OrderDate))
        , 0) AS [Product % Month Sales]
```

If you want to make your code easier to read, understand, and maintain, you can calculate all of the base aggregations in one pass in a common table expression (CTE) and then perform the second-order calculation in a following query, using the named result columns from the CTE instead of the expanded logic shown above. Once you have worked out the logic for any given combined calculation, you can comment out or remove the input columns and just return the final result columns that you are interested in. See Listing 9-4 for the code and Figure 9-3 for the results.

Listing 9-4. Base Query with Percent of Parent Calculations for [SalesAmount]

```
SELECT f.ProductKey,
    YEAR(f.orderdate) AS OrderYear,
    MONTH(f.orderdate) AS OrderMonth,
    SUM(f.SalesAmount) AS [Sales Amt],
    SUM(SUM(f.SalesAmount))
        OVER (PARTITION BY f.productkey)
        / SUM(SUM(f.SalesAmount))
            OVER() AS [Product % of All Sales],
    SUM(SUM(f.SalesAmount))
        OVER (PARTITION BY f.productkey, YEAR(f.OrderDate))
        / NULLIF(SUM(SUM(f.SalesAmount))
                OVER (PARTITION BY YEAR(f.OrderDate))
                ,0) AS [Product % Annual Sales],
    SUM(SUM(f.SalesAmount))
        OVER (PARTITION BY f.productkey, YEAR(f.OrderDate),
                MONTH(f.OrderDate))
        / NULLIF(SUM(SUM(f.SalesAmount))
                OVER (PARTITION BY YEAR(f.OrderDate), MONTH(f.OrderDate))
                ,0) AS [Product % Month Sales]
FROM dbo.FactInternetSales AS f
WHERE OrderDate BETWEEN '2011-01-01' AND '2012-12-31'
GROUP BY f.ProductKey,
        YEAR(f.orderdate),
        MONTH(f.orderdate)
ORDER BY 2, 3, f.ProductKey;
```

	ProductK...	OrderY...	OrderMo...	Sales Amt	Product % of All Sales	Product % Annual Sales	Product % Month Sales
1	310	2011	1	78721.94	0.0925	0.1689	0.1675
2	311	2011	1	78721.94	0.0775	0.1416	0.1675
3	312	2011	1	96613.29	0.0927	0.1694	0.2056
4	313	2011	1	53674.05	0.0833	0.1522	0.1142
5	314	2011	1	60830.59	0.0814	0.1486	0.1294
6	322	2011	1	699.0982	0.0009	0.0016	0.0014
7	324	2011	1	699.0982	0.0008	0.0015	0.0014
8	326	2011	1	1398.1964	0.0011	0.0021	0.0029

Figure 9-3. The results for Listing 9-4

Period-to-Date Calculations

Period-to-date calculations are a mainstay of financial reports, but are notoriously difficult to incorporate into query-based reports without resorting to multiple CTEs or temporary tables. Typically the grouping is performed in a reporting tool such as SSRS or Excel to provide the aggregated results, but this can be tricky to implement. The examples you will work through next will show you how to create multiple levels of rolling totals in a single result set, by adding a FRAME clause to the mix. The frame clause is covered in more detail in Chapter 6.

Listing 9-5 demonstrates how to use the frame definition to calculate period-to-date totals by date, by product for months, quarters, and years. The base query is essentially the same as before, but the level of granularity is at the date level instead of the month level. This is so that you can see the results of the aggregate columns in more detail.

Listing 9-5. Calculating Period-to-Date Running Totals By Date

```
--x.2.1 day level aggregates, with rolling totals for MTD, QTD, YTD
SELECT f.OrderDate, f.ProductKey,
       YEAR(f.orderdate) AS OrderYear,
       MONTH(f.orderdate) AS OrderMonth,
       SUM(f.SalesAmount) AS [Sales Amt],
       SUM(SUM(f.SalesAmount))
           OVER(PARTITION BY f.productkey, YEAR(f.orderdate),
                MONTH(f.orderdate)
                ORDER BY f.productkey, f.orderdate
                ROWS BETWEEN UNBOUNDED PRECEDING AND CURRENT ROW
               ) AS [Sales Amt MTD],
       SUM(SUM(f.SalesAmount))
       OVER(PARTITION BY f.productkey, YEAR(f.orderdate),
            DATEPART(QUARTER, f.OrderDate)
            ORDER BY f.productkey, YEAR(f.orderdate), MONTH(f.orderdate)
            ROWS BETWEEN UNBOUNDED PRECEDING AND CURRENT ROW
           ) AS [Sales Amt QTD],
       SUM(SUM(f.SalesAmount))
           OVER(PARTITION BY f.productkey, YEAR(f.orderdate)
           ORDER BY f.productkey, f.orderdate
           ROWS BETWEEN UNBOUNDED PRECEDING AND CURRENT ROW
           ) AS [Sales Amt YTD],
       SUM(SUM(f.SalesAmount))
           OVER(PARTITION BY f.productkey
           ORDER BY f.productkey, f.orderdate
           ROWS BETWEEN UNBOUNDED PRECEDING AND CURRENT ROW
           ) AS [Sales Amt Running Total],
FROM dbo.FactInternetSales AS f
GROUP BY f.orderdate, f.ProductKey, YEAR(f.orderdate), MONTH(f.orderdate)
ORDER BY f.ProductKey, f.OrderDate;
```

The OVER clause examples shown in Listing 9-5 use the ROWS BETWEEN UNBOUNDED PRECEDING AND CURRENT ROW frame. This results in the calculation aggregating all rows from the beginning of the frame to the current row, giving you the correct total to date for the level specified in the PARTITION clause. For instance, the [Sale Amt MTD] aggregate column will calculate the SUM([SalesAmount]) from the first day of the month, the first unbounded preceding row, through to the current row. The ORDER BY clause becomes mandatory when using a FRAME clause, otherwise there would be no context for the frame to be moved along within the PARTITION.

Figure 9-4 shows the partial results. The [Sales Amt MTD], [Sales Amt QTD], and [Sales Amt YTD] column values increase until reaching a different [ProductKey] or [ProductKey] and time level (Month and Quarter). The results in Figure 9-4 show the break in aggregations at the end of the second quarter, so you can see by looking at the rows where [ProductKey] is equal to 311, 312, or 313 that the aggregation resets on October 1.

	ProductKey	OrderDate	OrderYear	OrderQuarter	OrderMonth	Sales Amt	Sales Amt MTD	Sales Amt QTD	Sales Amt YTD
1152	311	2011-09-29 ...	2011	3	9	3578.27	108191.56	239744.09	737123.62
1153	312	2011-09-29 ...	2011	3	9	3578.27	110926.37	329200.84	869519.61
1154	313	2011-09-29 ...	2011	3	9	3578.27	75143.67	289839.87	758593.24
1155	028	2011-09-29 ...	2011	3	9	899.0982	899.0982	5582.7858	11854.8884
1156	340	2011-09-29 ...	2011	3	9	699.0982	2796.3928	6291.8838	7890.0802
1157	311	2011-09-30 ...	2011	3	9	3578.27	103769.83	243322.36	740701.89
1158	312	2011-09-30 ...	2011	3	9	3578.27	114504.64	332779.11	873097.88
1159	348	2011-09-30 ...	2011	3	9	3399.99	23799.93	37399.89	112199.67
1160	310	2011-10-01 ...	2011	4	10	7156.54	7156.54	7156.54	898145.77
1161	312	2011-10-01 ...	2011	4	10	7156.54	7156.54	7156.54	880254.42
1162	313	2011-10-01 ...	2011	4	10	3578.27	3578.27	3578.27	762171.51
1163	314	2011-10-01 ...	2011	4	10	7156.54	7156.54	7156.54	769328.05
1164	330	2011-10-01 ...	2011	4	10	899.0982	899.0982	899.0982	9787.3748
1165	351	2011-10-01 ...	2011	4	10	3374.99	3374.99	3374.99	111374.67
1166	311	2011-10-02 ...	2011	4	10	7156.54	7156.54	7156.54	747858.43
1167	312	2011-10-02 ...	2011	4	10	3578.27	10734.81	10734.81	883832.69
1168	313	2011-10-02 ...	2011	4	10	7156.54	10734.81	10734.81	769328.05

Figure 9-4. *Partial results at the end of a quarter (September 30th)*

Averages, Moving Averages, and Rate-of-Change

Before moving on to more involved examples, you need to stop and consider the challenges faced when working with dates. Dates as a data type are continuous and sequential. The T-SQL functions that work with dates are written with this in mind and handle any involved date math correctly. In reality, data based on dates will not be continuous. Transaction data will have gaps where there is no data for a day, week, or possibly even a month or more.

Window functions are not date aware, so it is up to you to ensure that any aggregate calculations handle gaps in the data correctly. If you use the LEAD() and LAG() window functions over date ranges or date period ranges, you have to provide partitions in your result sets that contain continuous and complete sets of dates, months, quarters, or years as needed by your calculations. Failure to do so will result in incorrect results. The reason for this is that the LEAD() and LAG() functions operate over the result set of the query, moving the specified number of rows forward or backwards in the result set, regardless of the number of days or months represented.

For example, a three-month rolling average implemented incorrectly using window functions won't take into account cases where there is no data for a product in a given month. It will perform the frame subset over the data provided and produce an average over the prior three months, regardless of whether they are contiguous months or not. Listing 9-6 demonstrates how not accounting for gaps in a date range will result in incorrect or misleading results. In this example, the data is being aggregated to the Month level by removing any grouping reference to [OrderDate].

Listing 9-6. Incorrectly Handing Gaps Dates

```
--9.7 Handling gaps in dates, Month level: not handling gaps
SELECT ROW_NUMBER()
      OVER(ORDER BY f.ProductKey, YEAR(f.OrderDate), MONTH(f.OrderDate))
      AS [RowID],
      f.ProductKey,
      YEAR(f.OrderDate) AS OrderYear,
      MONTH(f.OrderDate) AS OrderMonth,
      ROUND(SUM(f.SalesAmount), 2) AS [Sales Amt], -- month level
      ROUND(SUM(SUM(f.SalesAmount))
            OVER(PARTITION BY f.ProductKey, YEAR(f.OrderDate)
                 ORDER BY f.ProductKey, YEAR(f.OrderDate), MONTH(f.OrderDate)
                 ROWS BETWEEN UNBOUNDED PRECEDING AND CURRENT ROW
                 ), 2) AS [Sales Amt YTD],
      ROUND(AVG(SUM(f.SalesAmount))
            OVER(PARTITION BY f.ProductKey
                 ORDER BY f.ProductKey, YEAR(f.OrderDate), MONTH(f.OrderDate)
                 ROWS BETWEEN 3 PRECEDING AND CURRENT ROW
                 ),2) AS [3 Month Moving Avg]
FROM [dbo].[FactInternetSales] AS f
WHERE ProductKey = 332
AND f.OrderDate BETWEEN '2010-12-01' AND '2011-12-31'
GROUP BY f.ProductKey, YEAR(f.OrderDate), MONTH(f.OrderDate)
ORDER BY f.ProductKey ,YEAR(f.OrderDate), MONTH(f.OrderDate)
```

The results are shown in Figure 9-5; notice that for the time range selected, only nine months are represented. Calculating a moving average over the range of months that contain no data will produce incorrect results. You will learn how to address this next by filling in the gaps.

	RowID	ProductKey	OrderYear	OrderMonth	Sales Amt	Sales Amt YTD	3 Month Moving Avg
1	1	332	2011	1	2097.29	2097.29	2097.29
2	2	332	2011	4	1398.20	3495.49	1747.75
3	3	332	2011	5	699.10	4194.59	1398.20
4	4	332	2011	6	2796.39	6990.98	1747.75
5	5	332	2011	7	699.10	7690.08	1398.20
6	6	332	2011	8	1398.20	9088.28	1398.20
7	7	332	2011	9	699.10	9787.37	1398.20
8	8	332	2011	10	1398.20	11185.57	1048.65
9	9	332	2011	12	1398.20	12583.77	1223.42

Figure 9-5. *Incorrect calculation of a moving average*

In order to address this problem, a supplementary Date table needs to be used to fill in the gaps in the transaction data. This is not a new problem, and it has been solved in data warehouse designs by including a Date dimension table that contains a row for every date in a specified range of years. The AdventureWorksDW database contains a table called DimDate that will be used in the following examples. In the event that you do not have a date dimension at your disposal, you can also use a CTE to create a Date dimension table. The use of a table of date values will result in much better performance over using a CTE.

In Listing 9-7, the DimDate table is cross joined with the DimProduct table to produce a set containing all products for all dates in the specified range. The resulting CTE "table" is used as the primary table in the SELECT portion of the query so that every date in the range is represented in the aggregated results even if there were no transactions for that product in a given time period. You can also pick up additional attributes from the Product table such as product category, color, etc., row counts, and distinct counts from the fact table. These can be used to create additional statistics. In this case, [ProductAlternateKey] is added and takes the place of [ProductKey] in all grouping operations in order to make the results more user-friendly.

Listing 9-7. Correctly Handling Gaps in Dates

```
--9.7 month level. Now handling gaps in transaction dates
WITH CTE_ProductPeriod
AS (
    SELECT p.ProductKey, p.ProductAlternateKey as [ProductID],
        Datekey, CalendarYear,
        CalendarQuarter, MonthNumberOfYear AS CalendarMonth
    FROM DimDate AS d
    CROSS JOIN DimProduct p
    WHERE d.FullDateAlternateKey BETWEEN '2011-01-01' AND '2013-12-31'
    AND EXISTS(SELECT * FROM FactInternetSales f
            WHERE f.ProductKey = p.ProductKey
            AND f.OrderDate BETWEEN '2011-01-01' AND '2013-12-31')
)
```

```
SELECT ROW_NUMBER()
       OVER(ORDER BY p.[ProductID],
                    p.CalendarYear,
                    p.CalendarMonth
            ) as [RowID],
       p.[ProductID],
       p.CalendarYear  AS OrderYear,
       p.CalendarMonth AS OrderMonth,
       ROUND(SUM(COALESCE(f.SalesAmount,0)), 2) AS [Sales Amt],
       ROUND(SUM(SUM(f.SalesAmount))
                OVER(PARTITION BY p.[ProductID], p.CalendarYear
                     ORDER BY P.[ProductID], p.CalendarYear, p.CalendarMonth
                     ROWS BETWEEN UNBOUNDED PRECEDING AND CURRENT ROW
                ), 2) AS [Sales Amt YTD],
       ROUND(SUM(SUM(COALESCE(f.SalesAmount, 0)))
                OVER(PARTITION BY p.[ProductID]
                     ORDER BY p.[ProductID], p.CalendarYear, p.CalendarMonth
                     ROWS BETWEEN 3 PRECEDING AND CURRENT ROW
                ) / 3, 2) AS [3 Month Moving Avg]
FROM CTE_ProductPeriod AS p
LEFT OUTER JOIN [dbo].[FactInternetSales]  AS f
    ON p.ProductKey = f.ProductKey
    AND p.DateKey = f.OrderDateKey
WHERE p.ProductKey = 332
AND p.CalendarYear =  2011
GROUP BY p.[ProductID], p.CalendarYear, p.CalendarMonth
ORDER BY p.[ProductID], p.CalendarYear, p.CalendarMonth
```

The results are shown in Figure 9-6. Compare the results of the two previous queries. The [3 Month Moving Avg] column is now correct for the months where there were no sales for the product (Feb, Mar, Nov) and for the months immediately after the empty periods (May, June, December). The calculation in the second query did not use the AVG() function but rather divides the SUM() by three to arrive at the average. This ensures a more accurate average for the first three periods. In following sections you will learn how to limit calculations only to ranges that are complete when calculating moving averages.

	RowID	ProductID	OrderY...	OrderMo...	Sales A...	Sales Amt YTD	3 Month Moving Avg
1	1	BK-R50B-58	2011	1	2097.29	2097.29	699.10
2	2	BK-R50B-58	2011	2	0.00	2097.29	699.10
3	3	BK-R50B-58	2011	3	0.00	2097.29	699.10
4	4	BK-R50B-58	2011	4	1398.20	3495.49	1165.16
5	5	BK-R50B-58	2011	5	699.10	4194.59	699.10
6	6	BK-R50B-58	2011	6	2796.39	6990.98	1631.23
7	7	BK-R50B-58	2011	7	699.10	7690.08	1864.26
8	8	BK-R50B-58	2011	8	1398.20	9088.28	1864.26
9	9	BK-R50B-58	2011	9	699.10	9787.37	1864.26
10	10	BK-R50B-58	2011	10	1398.20	11185.57	1398.20
11	11	BK-R50B-58	2011	11	0.00	11185.57	1165.16
12	12	BK-R50B-58	2011	12	1398.20	12583.77	1165.16

Figure 9-6. *Moving average, taking gaps in sales data into account*

Same Period Prior Year

Part and parcel with providing period-to-date calculations, you will need to provide comparisons to the same period in the prior year, the prior period in the same year, and quite possibly difference amounts and difference percentages. These aggregates can be calculated in exactly the same way as the items you have work with so far: by defining the formula in simple terms, determining the input calculations at a column level, and then building the output column using the input calculations.

For this example, the [ProductKey] is dropped from the query so that the granularity of the results is at a month level. This makes it easier for you to see the effect of the new calculations in the smaller number of result rows. In order to calculate a value from a prior year, the query cannot be limited to a single year in the WHERE clause. For a window function to be able to look back into a prior year, there has to be more than one year available in the result set.

The LAG() function can retrieve and aggregate data by looking back in the record set by the number of rows specified. It also has an optional default parameter that can be used to return a zero value for cases where there is no row available when navigating back through the records. See Listing 9-8 for the code and Figure 9-7 for the results.

Listing 9-8. Retrieving Results for the Same Month of the Prior Year

```
-- Listing 9.8 Same Month Prior Year
WITH CTE_ProductPeriod
AS (
    SELECT p.ProductKey, --p.ProductAlternateKey as [ProductID],
        Datekey, CalendarYear, CalendarQuarter,
        MonthNumberOfYear AS CalendarMonth
    FROM DimDate AS d
    CROSS JOIN DimProduct p
        WHERE d.FullDateAlternateKey BETWEEN '2011-01-01' AND '2013-12-31'
```

```
        AND EXISTS(SELECT * FROM FactInternetSales f
                WHERE f.ProductKey = p.ProductKey
                AND f.OrderDate BETWEEN '2011-01-01' AND '2013-12-31')
    )
SELECT
    ROW_NUMBER()
        OVER(ORDER BY p.CalendarYear, p.CalendarMonth) as [RowID],
    p.CalendarYear AS OrderYear,
    p.CalendarMonth AS OrderMonth,
    ROUND(SUM(COALESCE(f.SalesAmount,0)), 2) AS [Sales Amt],
    ROUND(SUM(SUM(COALESCE(f.SalesAmount, 0)))
                OVER(PARTITION BY p.CalendarYear
                    ORDER BY p.CalendarYear, p.CalendarMonth
                    ROWS BETWEEN UNBOUNDED PRECEDING AND CURRENT ROW
                    ), 2) AS [Sales Amt YTD],
    ROUND(LAG(SUM(f.SalesAmount), 12 , 0)
            OVER(ORDER BY p.CalendarYear, p.CalendarMonth),2)
        as [Sales Amt Same Month PY]
FROM CTE_ProductPeriod AS p
LEFT OUTER JOIN [dbo].[FactInternetSales] AS f
    ON p.ProductKey = f.ProductKey
    AND p.DateKey = f.OrderDateKey
GROUP BY p.CalendarYear, p.CalendarMonth
ORDER BY p.CalendarYear, p.CalendarMonth
```

	RowID	OrderYear	OrderMonth	Sales Amt	Sales Amt YTD	Sales Amt Same Month PY
1	1	2011	1	469823.91	469823.91	0.00
2	2	2011	2	466334.90	936158.82	0.00
3	3	2011	3	485198.66	1421357.48	0.00
4	4	2011	4	502073.85	1923431.32	0.00
5	5	2011	5	561681.48	2485112.80	0.00
6	6	2011	6	737839.82	3222952.62	0.00
7	7	2011	7	596746.56	3819699.18	0.00
8	8	2011	8	614557.94	4434257.11	0.00
9	9	2011	9	603083.50	5037340.61	0.00
10	10	2011	10	708208.00	5745548.61	0.00
11	11	2011	11	660545.81	6406094.43	0.00
12	12	2011	12	669431.50	7075525.93	0.00
13	13	2012	1	495364.13	495364.13	469823.91
14	14	2012	2	506994.19	1002358.31	466334.90
15	15	2012	3	373483.01	1375841.32	485198.66

Figure 9-7. *Same month, prior year results*

Difference and Percent Difference

Once you have the ability to look back and pluck a value from the past, you can calculate differences between those values very easily. The commonly accepted method for calculating Percent Difference is ([current] - [previous]) / [previous]. You can also multiply the result by 100 if you want the percentage values to be in the format of ##.###. Add the code shown in Listing 9-9 to the query from Listing 9-8 to incorporate the calculations and run the query.

Listing 9-9. Difference: Current Month Over the Same Month of the Prior Year

```
LAG(SUM(f.SalesAmount), 12, 0 )
        OVER(ORDER BY p.CalendarYear, p.CalendarMonth)
   as [Sales Amt Same Month PY],
-- [Diff] = [CY] - [PY]
SUM(COALESCE(f.SalesAmount,0))
    - LAG(SUM(f.SalesAmount), 12, 0)
          OVER(ORDER BY p.CalendarYear, p.CalendarMonth)
   as [PY MOM Diff],
-- [Pct Diff] = ([CY] - [PY]) / [PY]
(SUM(COALESCE(f.SalesAmount,0))
    - LAG(SUM(f.SalesAmount), 12, 0)
          OVER(ORDER BY p.CalendarYear, p.CalendarMonth)
    ) / nullif(LAG(SUM(f.SalesAmount), 12, 0 )
          OVER(ORDER BY p.CalendarYear, p.CalendarMonth),0)
   as [PY MOM Diff %]
```

	RowID	OrderY...	OrderMo...	Sales Amt	Sales Amt YTD	Sales Amt Same Month PY	PY MOM Diff	PY MOM Diff %
1	1	2011	1	469823.91	469823.91	0.00	469823.91	NULL
2	2	2011	2	466334.90	936158.82	0.00	466334.90	NULL
3	3	2011	3	485198.66	1421357.48	0.00	485198.66	NULL
4	4	2011	4	502073.85	1923431.32	0.00	502073.85	NULL
5	5	2011	5	561681.48	2485112.80	0.00	561681.48	NULL
6	6	2011	6	737839.82	3222952.62	0.00	737839.82	NULL
7	7	2011	7	596746.56	3819699.18	0.00	596746.56	NULL
8	8	2011	8	614557.94	4434257.11	0.00	614557.94	NULL
9	9	2011	9	603083.50	5037340.61	0.00	603083.50	NULL
10	10	2011	10	708208.00	5745548.61	0.00	708208.00	NULL
11	11	2011	11	660545.81	6406094.43	0.00	660545.81	NULL
12	12	2011	12	669431.50	7075525.93	0.00	669431.50	NULL
13	13	2012	1	495364.13	495364.13	469823.91	25540.21	0.0543
14	14	2012	2	506994.19	1002358.31	466334.90	40659.28	0.0871
15	15	2012	3	373483.01	1375841.32	485198.66	-111715.65	-0.2302
16	16	2012	4	400335.61	1776176.93	502073.85	-101738.23	-0.2026

Figure 9-8. *Difference: current month over the same month of the prior year*

Figure 9-8 shows the results. The same approach can be used to determine the value for the prior month and the difference between it and the current month. Add the code from Listing 9-10 and run the query to calculate the prior month value, month-over-month difference, and month-over-month difference percentage. The results are shown in Figure 9-9.

Listing 9-10. Difference: Current Month Over the Same Month of the Prior Year

```
LAG(SUM(f.SalesAmount), 1, 0)
        over(ORDER BY p.CalendarYear, p.CalendarMonth) as [Sales Amt PM],
    -- [Difference] = [CM] - [PM]
        SUM(COALESCE(f.SalesAmount,0))
          - LAG(SUM(f.SalesAmount), 1, 0)
                over(ORDER BY p.CalendarYear, p.CalendarMonth)
        as [PM MOM Diff],
    -- [Pct Difference] = ([CM] - [PM]) / [PM]
(SUM(COALESCE(f.SalesAmount,0))
  - LAG(SUM(f.SalesAmount), 1, 0)
          OVER(ORDER BY p.CalendarYear, p.CalendarMonth))
        / nullif(LAG(SUM(f.SalesAmount), 1, 0 )
                OVER(ORDER BY p.CalendarYear, p.CalendarMonth),0)
        as [PM MOM Diff %]
```

	RowID	OrderY...	OrderMo...	Sales Amt	Sales Amt YTD	Sales Amt PM	PM MOM Diff	PM MOM Diff %
1	1	2011	1	469823.91	469823.91	0.00	469823.9148	NULL
2	2	2011	2	466334.90	936158.82	469823.9148	-3489.0118	-0.0074
3	3	2011	3	485198.66	1421357.48	466334.903	18863.7564	0.0404
4	4	2011	4	502073.85	1923431.32	485198.6594	16875.1864	0.0347
5	5	2011	5	561681.48	2485112.80	502073.8458	59607.63	0.1187
6	6	2011	6	737839.82	3222952.62	561681.4758	176158.3456	0.3136
7	7	2011	7	596746.56	3819699.18	737839.8214	-141093.2646	-0.1912
8	8	2011	8	614557.94	4434257.11	596746.5568	17811.3782	0.0298
9	9	2011	9	603083.50	5037340.61	614557.935	-11474.4374	-0.0186
10	10	2011	10	708208.00	5745548.61	603083.4976	105124.5056	0.1743
11	11	2011	11	660545.81	6406094.43	708208.0032	-47662.19	-0.0672
12	12	2011	12	669431.50	7075525.93	660545.8132	8885.6899	0.0134
13	13	2012	1	495364.13	495364.13	669431.5031	-174067.377	-0.26
14	14	2012	2	506994.19	1002358.31	495364.1261	11630.0615	0.0234
15	15	2012	3	373483.01	1375841.32	506994.1876	-133511.1822	-0.2633
16	16	2012	4	400335.61	1776176.93	373483.0054	26852.6091	0.0718

Figure 9-9. *Difference: current month to prior month*

Moving Totals and Simple Moving Averages

The complexity of the queries in this chapter has been building with each example. They are about to become even more complex. In order to help keep them understandable, you need to think about them conceptually as the number of "passes" the queries are taking over the data. The early examples were a single query, aggregating over a set of records in a single pass. In order to introduce a contiguous range of dates to eliminate gaps in the transaction data, a second pass was added by introducing a CTE to do some pre-work before the main aggregation query. In this section of the chapter, you will be adding a third pass by turning the aggregate from the last example into a CTE, and aggregating results on top of it. In some cases, the same results can be achieved with one or two passes, but for cases where nesting of a window function is required, the only option is to add another pass. One example of this is calculating [Sales Amt PY YTD] at the Month level. To create the [Sales Amt YTD] measure, you had to use all the clauses of the window function. There is no method to allow you to shift the partition back to the prior year. By first calculating [Sales Amt YTD] in the second pass, you can then use a window function in the third pass to calculate [Sales Amt PY YTD].

A secondary advantage is that the column calculations on any higher-order passes can use the meaningful column names from the lower-order passes to make the calculations easier to understand and the code more compact. Managing the trade-offs of performance and code readability has to be considered as well.

The last item that needs to be addressed is making sure the sets for any moving total or moving average calculation contain the correct number of input rows. For example, a three-month moving average [3 MMA] must contain data from three complete months, or it is not correct. By addressing gaps in transaction date ranges, part of the problem was solved but not the complete problem. At the beginning of a set, the first row has no prior rows, so it is incorrect to calculate a moving average for that row. The second row of the set only has one preceding row, making it incorrect to calculate the average for it as well. Only when the third row is reached are the conditions correct for calculating the three-month moving average. Table 9-1 shows how a three-month average should be calculated, given that the prior year had no data for the product.

Table 9-1. *Eliminating Incomplete Results for Averages Over Ranges of Periods*

Month	Product	Sales	Sales YTD	Sales 3 MMA
January	Bacon	1000	1000	
February	Bacon	500	1500	
March	Bacon	1500	3000	1000
April	Bacon	600	3600	867
May	Bacon	0	3600	700
June	Bacon	400	4000	333

To make this work, you simply have to count the number of rows in the frame for the three-month period instead of averaging the results, and use the count to determine when to perform the calculation. If there are three rows, perform the calculation; otherwise, return a null value. The following example uses a CASE statement to determine which rows have two preceding rows:

```
CASE WHEN COUNT(*) OVER (ORDER BY p.CalendarYear, p.CalendarMonth
             ROWS BETWEEN 2 PRECEDING AND CURRENT ROW) = 3
       THEN AVG(SUM(f.SalesAmount))
              OVER(ORDER BY p.CalendarYear, p.CalendarMonth
              ROWS BETWEEN 2 PRECEDING AND current row)
       ELSE null
   END AS [Sales Amt 3 MMA]
```

   The query in Listing 9-11 includes Moving Total and Moving Average calculations
for rolling 3 and rolling 12 month periods. These are implemented in the second order
CTE, so that the results are available for further manipulation in the third order
SELECT statement.

Listing 9-11. Updates to the Base Query

```
--9.11 Month level, no product. Handling gaps, All products, 3 "pass" query
WITH CTE_ProductPeriod
AS  (
    SELECT p.ProductKey, Datekey,
            CalendarYear, CalendarQuarter,
            MonthNumberOfYear AS CalendarMonth
    FROM DimDate AS d
    CROSS JOIN DimProduct p
    WHERE d.FullDateAlternateKey BETWEEN '2011-01-01' AND GETDATE()
    AND EXISTS(SELECT * FROM FactInternetSales f
                WHERE f.ProductKey = p.ProductKey
                AND f.OrderDate BETWEEN '2011-01-01' AND GETDATE())
        ),
CTE_MonthlySummary
AS (
    SELECT ROW_NUMBER()
            OVER(ORDER BY p.CalendarYear, p.CalendarMonth) AS [RowID],
        p.CalendarYear AS OrderYear,
        p.CalendarMonth AS OrderMonth,
        count(distinct f.SalesOrderNumber) AS [Order Count],
        count(distinct f.CustomerKey) AS [Customer Count],
        ROUND(SUM(COALESCE(f.SalesAmount,0)), 2) AS [Sales Amt],
        ROUND(SUM(SUM(COALESCE(f.SalesAmount, 0)))
                OVER(PARTITION BY p.CalendarYear
                    ORDER BY p.CalendarYear, p.CalendarMonth
                    ROWS BETWEEN UNBOUNDED PRECEDING AND CURRENT ROW
                    ), 2)
            AS [Sales Amt YTD],
        ROUND(LAG(SUM(f.SalesAmount), 11, 0 )
                OVER(ORDER BY p.CalendarYear, p.CalendarMonth), 2)
            AS [Sales Amt SP PY],
        ROUND(LAG(SUM(f.SalesAmount), 1, 0)
                OVER(ORDER BY p.CalendarYear, p.CalendarMonth), 2)
            AS [Sales Amt PM],
        CASE WHEN COUNT(*)
                OVER(ORDER BY p.CalendarYear, p.CalendarMonth
                    ROWS BETWEEN 2 PRECEDING AND CURRENT ROW) = 3
            THEN AVG(SUM(f.SalesAmount))
                OVER(ORDER BY p.CalendarYear, p.CalendarMonth
                    ROWS BETWEEN 2 PRECEDING AND current row)
            ELSE null
```

```
                END AS [Sales Amt 3 MMA],  -- 3 Month Moving Average
           CASE WHEN count(*)
                       OVER(ORDER BY p.CalendarYear, p.CalendarMonth
                            ROWS BETWEEN 2 PRECEDING AND current row) = 3
               THEN SUM(SUM(f.SalesAmount))
                       OVER(ORDER BY p.CalendarYear, p.CalendarMonth
                            ROWS BETWEEN 2 PRECEDING AND current row)
                  ELSE null
            END AS [Sales Amt 3 MMT],   -- 3 month Moving Total
           CASE WHEN COUNT(*)
                       OVER (ORDER BY p.CalendarYear, p.CalendarMonth
                             ROWS BETWEEN 11 PRECEDING AND CURRENT ROW) = 12
               THEN AVG(SUM(f.SalesAmount))
                       OVER(ORDER BY p.CalendarYear, p.CalendarMonth
                             ROWS BETWEEN 11 PRECEDING AND current row)
                  ELSE null
             END AS [Sales Amt 12 MMA], -- 12 Month Moving Average
           CASE WHEN count(*)
                       OVER(ORDER BY p.CalendarYear, p.CalendarMonth
                            ROWS BETWEEN 11 PRECEDING AND current row) = 12
               THEN SUM(SUM(f.SalesAmount))
                    OVER (ORDER BY p.CalendarYear, p.CalendarMonth
                            ROWS BETWEEN 11 PRECEDING AND current row)
             ELSE null
          END AS [Sales Amt 12 MMT]    -- 12 month Moving Total
FROM CTE_ProductPeriod AS p
LEFT OUTER JOIN [dbo].[FactInternetSales] AS f
    ON p.ProductKey = f.ProductKey
    AND p.DateKey = f.OrderDateKey
GROUP BY p.CalendarYear, p.CalendarMonth
)
SELECT [RowID],
    [OrderYear],
    [OrderMonth],
    [Order Count],
    [Customer Count],
    [Sales Amt],
    [Sales Amt SP PY],
    [Sales Amt PM],
    [Sales Amt YTD],
    [Sales Amt 3 MMA],
    [Sales Amt 3 MMT],
    [Sales Amt 12 MMA],
    [Sales Amt 12 MMT],
    [Sales Amt] - [Sales Amt SP PY] AS [Sales Amt SP PY Diff],
    ([Sales Amt] - [Sales Amt SP PY])
```

```
        / NULLIF([Sales Amt SP PY], 0) AS [Sales Amt SP PY Pct Diff ],
    [Sales Amt] - [Sales Amt SP PY] AS [Sales Amt PY MOM Diff],
    ([Sales Amt] - [Sales Amt PM])
        / NULLIF([Sales Amt PM], 0) AS [Sales Amt PY MOM Pct Diff]
FROM CTE_MonthlySummary
ORDER BY [OrderYear], [OrderMonth]
```

Notice how much simpler and readable the final select is. Because you encapsulated the logic behind the columns in the previous CTE, the resulting columns are also available to be used in another layer of window functions. The addition of the Moving Monthly Totals (MMT) and Moving Monthly Average (MMA) that were added to the summary provide a way to address seasonality in the data by averaging the monthly totals across a range of months. Moving Totals smooth out the volatility in seasonal/noisy data. They can also be used to calculate an annual Rate-of-Change (RoC), which can be used to identify trends and measure cyclical change.

You could not create a column for [Sales Amt YTD PY] until now. With the [Sales Amt YTD] column present in every row of the CTE, you can now use a window function to look back to the same period in the prior year and use it to calculate a difference between the current year to date and the prior year to date. Remember, even though you are working with a query that returns data at a month level, this technique works for date level results as well. Add the block of column calculations in Listing 9-12 to the new base query from Listing 9-11 and explore the results.

Listing 9-12. Same Period Prior Year to Date Calculations

```
LAG([Sales Amt YTD], 11,0)
    OVER(ORDER BY [OrderYear], [OrderMonth])
    AS [Sales Amt PY YTD],
[Sales Amt YTD] - LAG([Sales Amt YTD], 11,0)
                    OVER(ORDER BY [OrderYear], [OrderMonth])
    AS [Sales Amt PY YTD Diff],
([Sales Amt YTD] - LAG([Sales Amt YTD], 11,0)
                    OVER(ORDER BY [OrderYear], [OrderMonth]))
        /NULLIF(LAG([Sales Amt YTD], 11, 0)
                    OVER(ORDER BY [OrderYear], [OrderMonth]), 0)
    AS [Sales Amt PY YTD Pct Diff]
```

Because of the number of columns returned in this query, a chart makes more sense to demonstrate the results; see Figure 9-10. The whole purpose of creating the difference and difference percent calculations is to be able to use them to analyze the data for trends. Plotting the data in a chart is a great way to visualize the results and present them to business users.

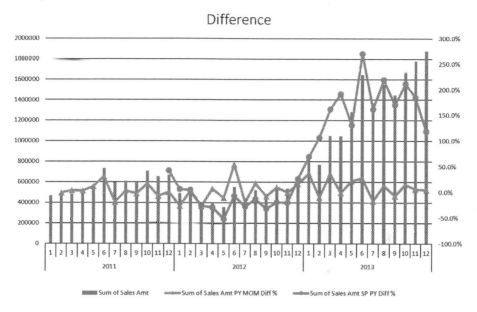

Figure 9-10. *Monthly trend chart showing Month over Month (MOM) difference percent and Same Period Previous Year (SP PY) difference precent*

MOM difference calculations are generally not that useful as a direct measure. They show the change from one period to the next, which can be very "noisy" and can hide underlying trends. SP PY difference calculations show a better picture of the growth trend over the prior year, but can also be prone to seasonality. That being said, you are now going to improve upon these calculations by implementing the Rate-of-Change calculations mentioned previously and smooth out the seasonal ups and downs into long-term trends.

Rate-of-Change Calculations

Rate-of-Change is the percentage of change in a Moving Total or Moving Average, and it indicates if a measure is improving over the prior year or getting worse. It is useful for determining leading and lagging indicators between divergent information sources. For example, if your business relies on petrochemical feedstock to produce its products, changes to oil prices are likely to presage a change in demand for your products, and could be considered a leading indicator. Charting the Rate-of-Change for corporate sales alongside the Rate-of-Change for stock market and commodity indices allows you to determine if your company's performance leads, lags, or is coincident with the performance of the stock market.

Add the code in Listing 9-13, a block of column calculations, to the query from Listing 9-11 and explore the results.

Listing 9-13. Rate-of-Change Calculations

```
--Rate of Change [3 MMT]/([3 MMT].LAG( 12 months))
[Sales Amt 3 MMT]
    / LAG(NULLIF([Sales Amt 3 MMT], 0), 11, null)
        OVER(ORDER BY [OrderYear], [OrderMonth])
    as [3/12 RoC],
--[12 MMT] /([12 MMT].LAG( 12 months))
[Sales Amt 12 MMT]
    / LAG(NULLIF([Sales Amt 12 MMT],0), 11, null)
        OVER(ORDER BY [OrderYear], [OrderMonth])
    as [12/12 RoC]
```

A RoC less than 1.0 (100%) is a downward trend and a RoC of 1.0 or greater is a positive change. The calculation can also be amended to turn the ratio into a positive or negative number as follows:

```
--Rate of Change +/- ([3 MMT]/([3 MMT].LAG( 12 months))* 100) -100
([Sales Amt 3 MMT] / LAG(NULLIF([Sales Amt 3 MMT], 0), 11, null)
            OVER(ORDER BY [OrderYear], [OrderMonth]) *100) - 100 as
            [3/12 RoC2],
--([12 MMT] /([12 MMT].LAG( 12 months))* 100) -100
    ([Sales Amt 12 MMT] / LAG(NULLIF([Sales Amt 12 MMT],0), 11, null)
            OVER(ORDER BY [OrderYear], [OrderMonth]) *100) - 100 as
            [12/12 RoC2]
```

The results of the Rate-of-Change calculations are best visualized in a chart; see Figure 9-11. In comparison to the chart for the difference percentages, you should notice a closer correlation of the [RoC] measures to the natural curve of the Total.

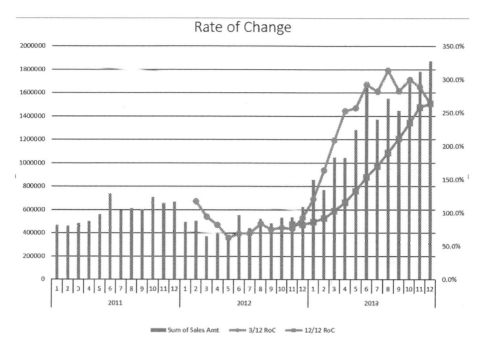

Figure 9-11. *Rate-of-Change trends for 3 and 12 month ranges*

Summary

This chapter covered a lot of ground, building on previously learned concepts to create complex calculations for time-based financial analysis. Some of the calculations were not previously easily accomplished in T-SQL, let alone in a single query. The approach of creating and validating input calculations before tackling more complex calculations will serve you well when developing your own complex window calculations, as will the step-wise method of using CTEs to get around the nesting limitation of window functions.

I hope you have realized just how versatile and powerful window functions are by reading this book. As you use these functions, you will begin to see even more ways to use them. They will change the way you approach queries, and you will become a better T-SQL developer. Happy querying!

Index

Get the eBook for only $10!

Now you can take the weightless companion with you anywhere, anytime. Your purchase of this book entitles you to 3 electronic versions for only $10.

This Apress title will prove so indispensible that you'll want to carry it with you everywhere, which is why we are offering the eBook in 3 formats for only $10 if you have already purchased the print book.

Convenient and fully searchable, the PDF version enables you to easily find and copy code—or perform examples by quickly toggling between instructions and   applications. The MOBI format is ideal for your Kindle, while the ePUB can be utilized on a variety of mobile devices.

Go to www.apress.com/promo/tendollars to purchase your companion eBook.